THE JEW OF VENICE

Borgo Press Books Edited & Translated by FRANK J. MORLOCK

Anna Karenina: A Play in Five Acts, by Edmond Guiraud, from Leo Tolstoy
Anthony: A Play in Five Acts, by Alexandre Dumas, Père
The Children of Captain Grant: A Play in Five Acts, by Jules Verne and Adolphe d'Ennery
Crime and Punishment: A Play in Three Acts, by Frank J. Morlock, from Fyodor Dostoyevsky
Don Quixote: A Play in Three Acts, by Victorien Sardou, from Miguel de Cervantes
The Dream of a Summer Night: A Fantasy Play in Three Acts, by Paul Meurice
Falstaff: A Play in Four Acts, by William Shakespeare, John Dennis, William Kendrick, and Frank J. Morlock
The Idiot: A Play in Three Acts, by Frank J. Morlock, from Fyodor Dostoyevsky
Jesus of Nazareth: A Play in Three Acts, by Paul Demasy
The Jew of Venice: A Play in Five Acts, by Ferdinand Dugué
Joan of Arc: A Play in Five Acts, by Charles Desnoyer
The Lily of the Valley: A Play in Five Acts, by Théodore Barrière and Arthur de Beauplan, from Honoré de Balzac
Lord Byron in Venice: A Play in Three Acts, by Jacques Ancelot
Louis XIV and the Affair of the Poisons: A Play in Five Acts, by Victorien Sardou
The Man Who Saw the Devil: A Play in Two Acts, by Gaston Leroux
Mathias Sandorf: A Play in Three Acts, by Jules Verne and William Busnach
Michael Strogoff: A Play in Five Acts, by Jules Verne and Adolphe d'Ennery
Les Misérables: A Play in Two Acts, by Victor Hugo, Paul Meurice, and Charles Victor Hugo
The Mysteries of Paris: A Play in Five Acts, by Eugène Sue and Prosper Dinaux
Ninety-Three: A Play in Four Acts, by Victor Hugo and Paul Meurice
Notes from the Underground: A Play in Two Acts, by Frank J. Morlock, from Fyodor Dostoyevsky
Outrageous Women: Lady MacBeth and Other French Plays, edited by Frank J. Morlock
Peau de Chagrin: A Play in Five Acts, by Louis Judicis, from Honoré de Balzac
A Raw Youth: A Play in Five Acts, by Frank J. Morlock, from Fyodor Dostoyevsky
Richard Darlington: A Play in Three Acts, by Alexandre Dumas, Père
The San Felice: A Play in Five Acts, by Maurice Drack, from Alexander Dumas, Père
Saul and David: A Play in Five Acts, by Voltaire
Shylock, the Merchant of Venice: A Play in Three Acts, by Alfred de Vigny
Socrates: A Play in Three Acts, by Voltaire
The Stendhal Hamlet Scenarios and Other Shakespearean Shorts from the French, edited by Frank J. Morlock
A Summer Night's Dream: A Play in Three Acts, by Joseph-Bernard Rosier and Adolphe de Leuwen
Urbain Grandier and the Devils of Loudon: A Play in Four Acts, by Alexandre Dumas, Père
The Voyage Through the Impossible: A Play in Three Acts, by Jules Verne and Adolphe d'Ennery
The Whites and the Blues: A Play in Five Acts, by Alexandre Dumas, Père
William Shakespeare: A Play in Six Acts, by Ferdinand Dugué

THE JEW OF VENICE

A PLAY IN FIVE ACTS

by

Ferdinand Dugué

Translated and Adapted by Frank J. Morlock

THE BORGO PRESS

An Imprint of Wildside Press LLC

MMX

CONTENTS

Cast of Characters 7

Prologue.. 9

Act I 33

Act II... 60

Act III 80

Act IV, Scene 1 96

Act IV, Scene 2 113

Act V 128

DEDICATION

TO

DON WOLOSHEN

CAST OF CHARACTERS

SHYLOCK

ANDRONICUS

HONORIUS

THE DOGE

ARNHEIM

AZZOLI

LEONE

UNALDO

JACOB

HEAD OF BRAVOS

LIGI

JACOPO

GINERVA

IMPERIA

SARAH

FABIA

PHOEBE

NINETTA

LORDS, COURTIERS, BRAVOS, GUARDS, PAGES, VALETS, NEGROES, BOATMEN, MEN OF THE PEOPLE, JEWS, ETC.

PROLOGUE

The stage is divided in two. To the right, Shylock's shop. To the left, a canal and bridge. Two men as if in ambush covered in cloaks and masks come and go on the bridge. At the rear a perspective of Venice. A side door leads from Shylock's shop to the canal via a staircase.

Night begins to fall.

RAFAEL: (to workers) Come on, come on, hurry a bit more; day is going to dawn and in business, as the master said, a minute is worth a million.

(to an errand boy) Your bales must be embarked this evening for the Morea; have them carried quickly to the Intrepid. Captain Andrca will help you with loading.

(to Workmen) Be careful, clumsy. If you do some damage we'll make you pay for it, be sure of that.

(Shylock enters with a Privateer)

SHYLOCK: (to the Privateer) No, no. No more time, it's

an impossible deal.

(The Privateer bows and leaves.)

(To an errand boy) Follow the Privateer who just left here and tell him I will take his merchandise; it's expensive and I will lose a lot of money, but the weather is rough and business is bad. So, in the end, I'll take it. Nonetheless, try to obtain some reduction.

(to another) Go get the amount due on these contracts, and without delay pursue those who do not pay. Ah, there are many cheats in Venice. Bring your scales to weight the coins.

(to another) You, run to the tax office to pay the duties on the last cargo received from Alexandria. The treasury, now that's a ruinous thing for merchants. My calculation doesn't run so high, before paying, verify the account.

(Shylock's orders are executed as he gives them.)

(approaching Rafael) Is this soon finished?

RAFAEL: Yes, Master. Here's the correspondence from Marseilles, London and Tunis.

SHYLOCK: Good, very good.

RAFAEL: I don't have anything to draw up but this.

SHYLOCK: From Palermo, right?

RAFAEL: Yes, Master.

SHYLOCK: Oh, that's the most important one. Pay attention, Rafael. Weight the value of each syllable before writing. Sicilian merchants find opportunities for chicanery in a missed accent or an extra comma.

LEONE: Hey, Shylock. Can't you see we are waiting for you?

SHYLOCK: I am yours, my dear lords, I am yours.

(to Rafael) Have you balanced the accounts for the last two weeks?

(to Leone) I beg you to take seats.

LEONE: It seems to me you should have offered them to us sooner.

SHYLOCK: Many excuses and a little patience.

LEONE: Wise guy!

SHYLOCK: Isn't patience a Christian virtue?

LEONE: By Saint Mark, you are insolent?

SHYLOCK: Not at all, my dear lords. I am doing business as you see.

LEONE: If I didn't control myself.

UBALDO: (low to Leone) He's pretty strong. Watch out.

LEONE: He'd better hurry up, at least, or I won't answer for myself.

SHYLOCK: (aside) When Shylock goes to the homes of the great lords they make him wait under the vestibule with the lackeys. Today, Shylock is taking his revenge.

(to Rafael) Have you got what I asked of you?

RAFAEL: Here's the picture of your operation, active and passive: There was an increase during the last two weeks.

SHYLOCK: Keep your voice down.

RAFAEL: An increase of 3000 ducats.

SHYLOCK: (intending to be heard) Business will end by becoming impossible and I will lose my last ducat. If these disasters continue I'll have to sell my business and open a booth on the corner of the plaza, and set myself up doing wholesale.

(to the lords) I am with you, my good lords, I am with you.

(to Rafael) Give me your pen so I can sign. Go now, expedite these letters.

(Rafael leaves, Jacob enters)

LEONE: Is it our turn finally?

SHYLOCK: Yes, my gentle lords.

LEONE: Thanks a bunch.

SHYLOCK: Hey, evening, neighbor Jacob.

JACOB: Evening, colleague.

(taking him aside) I want to speak to you briefly.

SHYLOCK: Speak, neighbor.

(to Leone) You'll excuse me? This will be short, very short.

LEONE: Ah! S'Death!

UBALDO: (low to Leone) No anger. We'll only lose by it.

JACOB: A magnificent opportunity is presenting itself, but a lack of money to conclude it, and only you have the ability.

SHYLOCK: Is the deal as good as you say?

JACOB: I'll answer for that, and without you, the Christian merchants are going to carry it off.

SHYLOCK: The Christian merchants—

JACOB: Yes.

SHYLOCK: Go back to the Rialto. I won't delay rejoining you.

(Jacob leaves)

Forgive me, Signor Ubaldo, and you, too, Signor Leone, but I am expected at the Rialto. Assuredly, it's a poor thing, a puny thing to accomplish, but what do you want? In business, you must use all kinds of wood to make a fire.

LEONE: Are you playing with us?

SHYLOCK: Oh! Could you think?

UBALDO: (to Leone) Let me talk, and you, bite your mustache.

SHYLOCK: Doubtless you are bringing me the money that you owe me. Marvelous! I am going to receive it, count it, put it in the safe, and discharge you of your obligations. Nothing simpler.

UBALDO: We are not bringing you a crown.

SHYLOCK: You want to have a laugh.

UBALDO: Not the least in the world.

SHYLOCK: Excuse me, there, on your note above your noble signature: "I will pay on such a day". That day has come and as I don't imagine that Venetian and Christian gentlemen can fail in their word to a poor Jew, I open my hand confidently.

UBALDO: And I solemnly place my purse here. For goodness sake it is empty. Come, don't be annoyed. What do you expect? The Carnival this winter was more voracious than usual; it swallowed everything, my good Shylock.

SHYLOCK: Ah, I am your good Shylock!

UBALDO: Our excellent Shylock, right, Leone?

SHYLOCK: Still, as of yesterday, not later than yesterday, your mistresses called me a dog from the height of your balcony; you had your valets throw mud at me, and your greyhounds gave chase!

UBALDO: A trifle! We were drunk.

SHYLOCK: And you no longer are?

UBALDO: We are less so.

SHYLOCK: Then you'll understand better what I have to tell you.

UBALDO: Look, give us a year's respite.

SHYLOCK: In quite precise legal terms your notes bears that you engage to the lender as guaranty of the sum counted to your hands, you chevalier Ubaldo, your villa at Trieste, you Marquis Leone, your palace on the Square of Saint Mark. Thus, since I am not reimbursed, I will have the villa and the palace sold to my profit without any delay.

LEONE: Miserable Jew.

SHYLOCK: Behold good Shylock has become miserable.

UBALDO: You couldn't be so harsh.

SHYLOCK: Yes! I gave you my word and I am going to keep it.

LEONE: My father's palace!

UBALDO: My last villa.

SHYLOCK: So much the worse for you! I am in my legal rights and I'm staying there. I'm not the one who did it. But since it protects me in passing, I'm profiting by it. Let's reason a bit and I'll give you an account of our respective positions. You, gentlemen, are the off shoots of the most noble and ancient Venetian families. As for me, I am a pariah, a miscreant, a leper, a Jew. You are powerful, respected, obeyed; I am insulted, scorned, hunted, almost a slave, still under threat of exile or prison, and your republic sells me, for the price of gold, the right to live. In a word, we have neither the same origin nor the same faith and the name brother wasn't meant for us! Why spare those who don't spare me? Why would I have in my heart pity for the enemies of my race? Come on, you have too much wit not to understand that it is impossible, and that I would be a dupe to act otherwise. Drive me out, imprison me, kill me if you are the stronger, but don't ask mercy of me when I have you in my hands! On that, I am leaving you. I'm expected on the Rialto.

UBALDO: If we offered you as an indemnity, higher interest?

SHYLOCK: I don't want it.

UBALDO: Why, you are enraged then?

SHYLOCK: It's possible.

LEONE: Ubaldo, let's not argue any further, and let's pay him.

SHYLOCK: What?

LEONE: With blows of a stick, praise God!

SHYLOCK: Marquis!

LEONE: Get your back ready, Jew!

SHYLOCK: I am in my home.

LEONE: You are in Venice!

SHYLOCK: Why that's dastardly; I am unarmed.

LEONE: So are dogs.

SHYLOCK: Dogs have teeth.

LEONE: So what?

SHYLOCK: Get out!

LEONE: Get your back ready, Jew!

SHYLOCK: If you hit me, I'll bite your face!

UBALDO: I told you he was enraged.

LEONE: Let's see about that.

(Leone hits him, Shylock rushes at him; Ubaldo stops him)

UBALDO: All vain, Master Shylock.

LEONE: You were speaking of the law just now. There's

one in Venice by which all threats against a Christian are punished by prison and amends; we are going now to bear a complaint before a magistrate and you will be arrested by tonight.

SHYLOCK: But you hit me!

UBALDO: Right, right, you will defend yourself before the court. Why the Devil are you so hard in business?

LEONE: (to Ubaldo) You see plainly, my dear, that blows with a stick are still the best policy.

UBALDO: Let's run to the magistrate.

(They leave)

JACOPO (to Luigi) The two gentlemen just left. There's no one else in the Jew's house.

LUIGI: And night is going to fall.

JACOPO: Arnheim's not here yet.

LUIGI: I hear the gondola.

JACOPO: About time.

SHYLOCK: I am a ninny. I lacked prudence and I may repent of it. The absurd reaction of rage. As if I had the right to be dignified over so small a matter, a blow with a stick! You must offer your spine and put it on the account with the rest. When will I be strong enough to remain mute under insult, to prevent my blood from boiling, to obliterate my face like that of a cadaver, to keep all my hate enchained at the bottom of my heart! Patience, I will succeed!

(The gondola ridden by Arnheim appears under the bridge)

ARNHEIM: (to gondolier) Stop! Let's stay a minute hidden under the arch,

JACOPO: (on the bridge) We are here.

ARNHEIM: Well?

JACOPO: Shylock's going to leave for the Rialto.

ARNHEIM: Let's wait, comrades. And no noise because the fox is clever.

(to Luigi and Jacopo) The rest of you continue to keep watch.

JACOPO: Don't worry.

SHYLOCK: I'm still going to take my precautions in case I'm arrested. Those accursed ones are capable of anything.

(calling) Sarah! Sarah!

SARAH: (entering) Here I am, Master.

SHYLOCK: What about my son?

SARAH: He just went to sleep, calm and smiling. One of his little hands folded under his cheek, and the other hangs the length of his cradle with a grace that calls for kisses.

SHYLOCK: He's handsome.

SARAH: Like Abel and Moses.

SHYLOCK: Lord, protect this child who no longer has a mother. You have taken back the companion I was given and I bend my face before your justice. Dear wife, she was too weak to struggle and I buried her furtively on the soil of exile! If this victim has not expiated my sins, strike me with lightning but spare my son! I've expended on him all that I have of tenderness and devotion for his mother; he's the only bond that ties me to life, the only hope which makes me believe in the future; without this immense love there'd be nothing human in my heart and that would be horrible! God of Abraham, take pity on me!

SARAH: Master, I join my humble prayer to yours.

SHYLOCK: Thanks, my good Sarah, you are not simply a vulgar serving wench, you are almost a sister to me, almost a mother to my son.

SARAH: I would be indeed ungrateful not to love you

thus, because the day when my husband abandoned me like a coward, you offered me food and an asylum. That was five years ago, but my gratitude has only increased.

SHYLOCK: That infamous fellow! You've forgotten him, completely forgotten him, haven't you?

SARAH: I remember him only in my prayers.

SHYLOCK: That's still too much, woman, because he has renounced our faith, that wretch. Stained by crime and debauchery! They say he died in the Indies, and truly, that's the best thing for him to do.

ARNHEIM: (aside) He's not done with it. Perchance could he be cajoling his serving wench? That would be very amusing.

SARAH: You are leaving, Master; have you orders to give me?

SHYLOCK: Listen, my faithful Sarah; I've just had a quarrel with two Venetian nobles, and it is possible I will be arrested.

SARAH: My God!

SHYLOCK: Imprisoned, even. Sarah, I am confiding my child to you.

SARAH: Master, count on me, but I hope that such a misfortune will not strike you.

SHYLOCK: In Venice there's nothing to hope for, everything to fear. Now, I'm running to find Jacob and put my last hours of freedom to profit. Gold, heaps of gold! Bring it, Christians, bring it! The Jews' strong-box is insatiable. Shylock intends that his son shall be rich like an emperor— Don't forget to make your rounds and to lock the bolts.

SARAH: Don't worry, Master.

SHYLOCK: Don't expect me in less than an hour.

(Shylock leaves)

SARAH: Let's see first of all if he's still sleeping.

(Sarah looks into the room on the right)

JACOPO: (to Arnheim) Shylock said: Don't expect me in less than an hour.

ARNHEIM: Marvelous.

LUIGI: He's getting further and further off.

ARNHEIM: Which way?

JACOPO: Towards the Rialto.

ARNHEIM: Great!

JACOPO: He's disappeared.

ARNHEIM: A short row to the stairs. (he leaps from the gondola onto the steps) Ah, I let the skeleton key fall. Pass it up to me.

SARAH: Dear little one, what purity, what an angelic smile. The merchandise has been unloaded, and the canal door might not be locked! (listening) That's strange! I just experienced something like a shiver of fear. Come on.

(Arnheim opens the door and finds himself face to face with Sarah who screams when she sees him)

ARNHEIM: Good evening, Madame Arnheim.

SARAH: God of Israel!

ARNHEIM: Er, yes, it's me, my sweet dove; Arnheim, your husband. My arrival is a little abrupt, but what do you want? I love to surprise folks.

SARAH: You! You! What are you coming here to do?

ARNHEIM: Sit down so we can chat.

SARAH: Help! Help!

(Luigi and Jacopo come through the back. Two other bravos half open the side door)

SARAH: Those men!

ARNHEIM: Fine, fine, comrades. Madame merely wanted to see if you were at your posts. Now she'll shut up!

JACOPO: That's what I'd advise her to do.

(The bravos move away.)

ARNHEIM: We won't be disturbed and you can be certain they'll keep a sharp guard around us. By the way, give me something to drink. I'm as thirsty as a sponge.

SARAH: Nothing in this house belongs to me.

ARNHEIM: Indeed. I'll do better to serve myself. (taking a bottle and a glass from a credenza)

SARAH: I'm not awake. I'm under the influence of a horrible dream.

ARNHEIM: Sit down, will you! Ah, I insist on it.

(filling his glass) To your health.

(drinks)

Pouah! Idiot of a miser! This is juice— You're a bit astonished to see me again, and no question you are counting, as soon as you pull yourself together a bit, on raining a deluge of reproaches on my head. Mercy, spare me these tender insults. You would be wrong. But I'm getting to the point. A few years ago in Smyrna, I made the acquaintance of a Greek, a charming man, we worked together, and thanks to a mutual sympathy, I was promptly honored with his confidence. The world, which has the most ridiculous prejudices against the noble profession of sea-rover, had an equally false idea of his physique. For to idlers, one cannot be a corsair except on the condition of having a Herculean face, a bull's voice, wild eyes, and enormous mustaches. Far from that, my friend was a fair adolescent with all the feminine graces and more than one duchess has envied the down on his lips, his pearly teeth, and rosy fingernails. For these excellent reasons, he seduced well and often the daughters of the richest merchants of the city. One good man became demented, threatened, tempted, tore his hair. But the dishonor was so public that he was forced to consent to a marriage and come what will. We were, with the father-in law if not more honest, at least, more legal. The honey moon of the newly-weds was, like ours, it couldn't have been shorter. And one day the poor woman died of a bad cold at three in the afternoon. But she had taken care to leave us a pretty brat who was worth several millions. This is full of interest, right?

SARAH: Continue. I've recovered my calm and I am listening.

ARNHEIM: I said the brat was worth several millions, and you must understand why. He became the direct heir of his grandfather. So, I leave you to imagine with what care we surrounded him. Suddenly, after a long voyage, we were going to leave the Adriatic to return to Smyrna, this bad monkey played us the trick of falling ill and dying in the blink of an eye. We were in a fix! To lose the wife, spilled ink, but to lose the child was another story. No possible inheritance. The Croesus who already had very little affection for his son-in-law would be eager to shut his door in his face, saying. "All our bonds are broken, you've become a stranger to me again. Go get yourself hanged, somewhere else." Luckily, my friend is a man of expedients who never loses his presence of mind in the most profound sorrow. He had a sudden inspiration, rapped me on the shoulder and said in this manner, "Arnheim, we are but a vile dust, let's give to my son the sepulcher of a sailor, let's keep his death a secret, and quickly find me somewhere a child of his age who will resemble him a bit. We'll take him to Smyrna. The grandfather won't see the trap and the ducats will be ours." It was a master stroke and I undertook the burden of the expedition. I climbed in a gondola, and I had myself taken to land after having first thrown the cadaver out a port-hole with a stone around its neck like a young cat.

SARAH: Monsters!

ARNHEIM: Now those are prejudices of which I was speaking just now. A clever man is never a monster. Once debarked, I lost myself in quest of an infant of three or four and as perseverance is one of my virtues, I ended by finding one.

SARAH: Ah!

ARNHEIM: A jewel of a child.

SARAH: Where was that?

ARNHEIM: Right here.

SARAH: The son of Shylock?

ARNHEIM: Yes.

SARAH: Truly?

ARNHEIM: I intend to make the fortune of the young pagan.

SARAH: And you imagined that unresisting, I would let you steal the child of my benefactor? Try it, why don't you!

ARNHEIM: Be sweet, my darling, be sweet.

SARAH: Before getting to him you will have to pass through my body.

ARNHEIM: Look, look, let's not get carried away. Anger is a villainous sin. Besides, my nerves are very sensitive tonight. You must understand. I have very sensitive nerves. You ought to understand that in addition to my attractions I am bringing an unshakable will, and it's not worth the trouble resisting me. So let me pass.

SARAH: Never.

ARNHEIM: Sarah, no childishness.

(walking towards her)

SARAH: Would you be cowardly enough to raise a hand against a woman?

ARNHEIM: Ah, fie then.

(calling) Come to me, the rest of you.

(he points her out to Jacopo and Luigi, who seize her and stifle her screams. Arnheim rushes into the chamber at the right.)

JACOPO: Zounds, what a woman!

LUIGI: She's got a strong wish to scream.

(Arnheim returns with the sleeping child)

ARNHEIM: The way I'm carrying him, I was born to be the father of a family.

(he crosses rapidly and descends to the gondola)

JACOPO: A noise of steps. It's Shylock returning.

LUIGI: This woman's going to talk.

JACOPO: She'll be quiet.

(he stabs Sarah who falls dead, and runs to the gondola with Jacopo) My word, Arnheim, you're a widower.

ARNHEIM: Quick, get out of here.

(They disappear under the bridge.)

SHYLOCK: I've managed to escape the bailiffs and I'm coming to hug my child one more time! Sarah!

(seeing her) Dead! Murdered! And my child!

(he leaps into the room and quickly returns in despair) My child, my poor little child. This open door. The water agitated by a gondola. Ah, curse on me! They've stolen him from me! They've torn my heart out!

(letting himself collapse on the steps of the stairway) O race of tigers!

(The officers of the police arrive with Leone and Ubaldo)

OFFICER: Don't worry, Milord Marquis. Justice will be done.

LEONE: (aside to Ubaldo) The Jew won't sell our treasure in such a hurry.

OFFICER: Hola, Shylock!

LEONE: A body?

SHYLOCK: I am not a citizen of your republic, but I pay tribute to Venice and Venice owes me protection. Some scoundrels have got in to my house tonight, they've killed my faithful serving woman, and carried off my only son. They must be pursued, slaughtered, torn to pieces, and my treasure returned.

OFFICER: There will be an inquest. They will decide.

SHYLOCK: Wait! Time is wasting and the wake of the oars is vanishing, and my life can break. No, no, I don't want to wait. Let the Magistrate keep his spies and his bailiffs. The wild beasts don't wait to tear their children from ravishers. They have their instincts, and that suffices them. I will do as they. All that I ask of you is an hour of liberty.

OFFICER: Impossible.

SHYLOCK: Impossible! But the quarrel with these gentlemen is nowhere near the misfortune which overwhelms me.

OFFICER: I'm here to arrest you, and I must arrest you. The rest does not concern me.

SHYLOCK: In that case you must have no children?

OFFICER: On the contrary.

SHYLOCK: And you love them?

OFFICER: That question—

SHYLOCK: (aside) I thought that fathers must always understand each other. I was mistaken. So much the better after all.

OFFICER: Indeed. You are not the one who struck this woman are you?

SHYLOCK: Me!

OFFICER: This knife doesn't belong to you?

SHYLOCK: This knife! Do I use weapons like this? Here, there's a Cross on the blade!

(aside) Ah, these are Christians!

OFFICER: To prison, Jew.

ALL: To prison!

SHYLOCK: So be it! But I shall return!

CURTAIN

ACT I

The garden of the courtesan Imperia. The end of a magnificent meal. The Decameron in full orgy.

AT RISE, pages and lackeys come and go. Bursts of laughter and the clinking of glasses. Gaming tables left and right.

ALL: Drink, drink.

IMPERIA: Now, Azzoli, a song.

ALL: Yes, yes,

PHOEBE: If, for splendid suppers there's only one Imperia in the world, there's only one Azzoli for happy tunes.

ALL: Let's listen, let's listen.

AZZOLI: (singing)

Already the dawn is shining and gleaming. Night is over.

Mistress, the enchanting hour passes and flies.
At your decree, I must surrender!
Leave, jealous one!
Let's hurry.
We must go down without waking her old husband!
Now our gondola
Discreetly steals
To the other shore.
Hurry, rowers! Let your oars
Slide on the blades
Without noise, without effort
Less strongly.

CHORUS:

Fie! To morose preachers
Who live too long.
Friends, with these roses
Let's let our twenty years bloom.

AZZOLI:

Feasts take after love in its turn
Mistress,
Give us intoxication
All day long.
Shame on those who, weary with drink
Have gone pale.
Vain care
Dark sorrow
Drown it all in this full cup.

Cup in hand, pour comrades!
Pour bumpers.
Over the shore.
Let a thundering and scolding refrain take wing
For the next world
And awake the dead.
More strongly!

CHORUS:

Fie on morose preachers
Who live too long!
Friends, with these roses
Let our twenty years bloom.

UBALDO: Azzoli, in your song there's a point of irony against me.

IMPERIA: How's that?

UBALDO: The refrain says: Let our twenty years bloom. And I joined in the chorus with the others, but what the devil, I've passed forty. Bah! What consoles me is that everyone isn't certain of making it there.

AZZOLI: It's a direction we're heading in: a man of forty will soon be a phenomenon; they will exhibit him in a cage like a new Methuselah.

(to a woman) Ninetta, a pill.

(he coughs)

UBALDO: (low to Imperia) Poor Azzoli.

IMPERIA: (the same) Poor Ninetta, rather. Come, my joyous guests. Let's each have a last toast. Begin with Honorius.

HONORIUS: To love!

IMPERIA: To luxury!

UBALDO: To Imperia, praise God!

ALL: To Imperia.

JEPPO: (approaching Honorius) Lord?

HONORIUS: Andronicus is not ill?

JEPPO: No, Lordship. Here's a letter.

HONORIUS: (after having read it) That's well, Jeppo. Greet you master on my behalf.

(Jeppo leaves)

He won't come to this fest. He doesn't blame me for being here, but his mere absence is a reproach to me. Well, he's wrong and he understands life ill. Pleasure must take place above all! Besides, is it my fault if I can live only here?

IMPERIA: (low to Ubaldo) Chevalier, distance yourself a bit with our friends.

(pointing to Honorius) I have to speak to him.

UBALDO: A walking tour of the games.

(to Azzoli) You are coughing frightfully, my dear. Go put yourself to bed.

AZZOLI: That's what I'm going to do.

UBALDO: Take your pills with you but leave us Ninetta.

NINETTA: It's agreed right?

AZZOLI: Not at all, not at all.

(to Ninetta) Support your lord and master.

UBALDO: And this drink is to the death of six uncles!

(they leave in different directions)

IMPERIA: That letter made you sad.

HONORIUS: You are mistaken, dear beauty.

IMPERIA: It was a woman who wrote you?

HONORIUS: No.

IMPERIA: Give me it.

(taking the letter and opening it) Ah, this proud Andronicus still refuses to come. Do you know what's preventing him?

HONORIUS: Business, no doubt.

IMPERIA: Say his scorn for the courtesan Imperia! Well, if he scorns me, I hate him and want to do him ill.

HONORIUS: That would be doing ill to me.

IMPERIA: So you love him so much?

HONORIUS: Hold it, Imperia. To convince you of it, I want to tell you how this friendship was formed. We were both born in Smyrna, we were the same age and our fathers got rich in commerce, died within a few days of each other, leaving us orphans quite young: Education, troubles, pleasure, all were common between us, and we grew up, side by side, like two twin brothers. Our characters alone, differed. I was ebullient, expansive, prodigal, avid of emotion and enjoyment, Andronicus, to the contrary had a rather cold benevolence, a smile sad enough and when he rested with his figures, it was to follow some dream through the mists of the horizon. At sixteen, he fitted out his vessels, opened his counters: he possessed credit throughout Europe, as for me, I was what I always will be, a loafer. Not being able to overcome my aversion to business, he associated me secretly in his profits. And without him, I'd have been ruined long ago, but that's not all. I had a quarrel with a Genoan bravo, I received a sword blow which put me out of combat, and it was agreed it would start over once I was cured. What did Andronicus do? He went to provoke the bravo and killed him; then he returned to care for me with tenderness without leaving my bedside day or night, without saying more to me than simple, touching words. "I wanted to be sure you would be here!" Ah, if one day I should be able to die for him that's all I ask of heaven.

IMPERIA: It's very romantic, that's certain.

HONORIUS: A short time later his business interests forced him to leave Smyrna; he came to establish himself in Venice and I followed him.

IMPERIA: He passes for the richest merchant in town.

HONORIUS: With good reason.

IMPERIA: He isn't loved by his colleagues, especially the Jews.

HONORIUS: Because he practices no usury, and fights it with all his strength! The probity of Andronicus causes the admiration of honest people, and the Doge himself has the highest esteem for him.

IMPERIA: I was wrong. A question still? If you had to choose between him and me?

HONORIUS: I love you ardently, Imperia but I think I told you I would be happy to die for him.

IMPERIA: Just so. Let's not speak of it any more. Do you know how much his fortune amounts to?

HONORIUS: No.

IMPERIA: You are not curious? Truly? I am annoyed that he shuns me in this way. I would take great pleasure in meeting him.

HONORIUS: I don't despair yet of bringing him to you, and I intend that in seeing you so beautiful, so resplendent, he shall grasp by what chains I am attached to you.

IMPERIA: Aren't you afraid he will become amorous of me?

HONORIUS: I don't fear him.

IMPERIA: Why's that?

HONORIUS: Because he loves elsewhere.

IMPERIA: Where might that be?

HONORIUS: I don't know her.

IMPERIA: Oh, you are discreet.

HONORIUS: I don't know her, I tell you. If he deserves a reproach, it's for not confiding himself to me without reserve.

IMPERIA: You are not worthy of it.

HONORIUS: (aside) Indeed.

IMPERIA: Such sanctuaries must not open to the profane!

HONORIUS: Andronicus must have chosen a noble creature.

IMPERIA: Who's worth more than me, I don't doubt. Do you want me to paint her portrait for you? She's a big girl, straight like a candle, and then from her collar straight to her eyebrows, set on a spring, with big feet, long arms and reddish hands; she was born under a counter, she had a scolding mother, and an idiot father, she sings off tune in a way that would make a cat howl. Her unique talent is to lower her eyes at everything, and I bet that each evening they hang all her clothes on a crochet nail in an armoire. You are not laughing? Decidedly, my dear, are you ill? Becoming virtuous? Bored with me? I warn you that I don't love lugubrious people and that I hold sadness in horror.

(taking his arm) By the way, aren't you a bit short on money?

HONORIUS: Have I refused you something?

IMPERIA: No. But I supposed. I've heard—

HONORIUS: What?

IMPERIA: That you owe two thousand ducats to Shylock that implacable Jew.

HONORIUS: I'm set to pay him.

IMPERIA: So much the better! Beside, one does not have friends for nothing. Your generous Andronicus might be able to loan them to you.

HONORIUS: I would never have recourse to him. I've wearied his good nature enough already.

IMPERIA: You see plainly you are bothered!

HONORIUS: What do you mean?

IMPERIA: It matters a lot to me.

HONORIUS: Why?

IMPERIA: I have a fantasy to satisfy.

HONORIUS: Dispose of me.

IMPERIA: Oh, no. It's something impossible.

HONORIUS: There's nothing impossible for the one who

loves you.

IMPERIA: Come on, you're being gallant again.

HONORIUS: It's a question of some jewel?

IMPERIA: Perhaps.

HONORIUS: Speak.

IMPERIA: Some other time! I need to consider again, but promise me to give me what I shall ask of you.

HONORIUS: Surely!

IMPERIA: Promising isn't swearing.

HONORIUS: I swear it to you.

IMPERIA: My dear Honorius, you are a charming man.

(Joyous tumult outside)

UBALDO: My word, my turtle doves, so much the worse if I interrupt your private chat, but this scatterbrain of a Leone just committed such an incredible buffoonery.

LEONE: (entering) Wait a moment, my friends, I am going to announce you.

(to Imperia) Good evening, Goddess.

IMPERIA: I'm angry with you, Marquis, for not having been one of us.

LEONE: I was behaving myself.

IMPERIA: Then they were more important hosts, since you preferred them.

LEONE: Surely.

IMPERIA: Look.

LEONE: I got all my creditors in a fraternal banquet.

IMPERIA: For goodness sake.

LEONE: Judge if we were numerous. Yes, all, from my tailor to the usurer Shylock.

ALL: Shylock!

IMPERIA: What! Shylock was seated at your table.

LEONE: By Jove, he didn't miss the opportunity to gorge himself at the expense of a Christian.

IMPERIA: You made him eat pork?

LEONE: Without his suspecting it; he found out later and ground his teeth like an ape.

UBALDO: That's not the best joke, Marquis. You are wrong to play with that man. This Shylock has an infernal look about him.

IMPERIA: (to Leone) Keep talking.

LEONE: I gave my comedians a meal worthy of Sardana-paulus, with lute players, heaps of flowers, with Blacka-moors and princely vessels. I dazzled them with my lack-eys and overwhelmed them with my attentions; I caressed their vanity by making them my equal, In short, I got them drunk in the most outrageous manner,

IMPERIA: And then?

LEONE: And then I brought them to your place.

IMPERIA: My place?

LEONE: Completely besotted.

IMPERIA: Good God! What do you want me to do with these cads?

LEONE: Wait. I have my plan. We are going to, will they, nil they, sit at a gambling table, and if after an hour we haven't despoiled them, I consent to lose my title and my name!

IMPERIA: Marvelous!

LEONE: Honorius, as it's you who owe Shylock the most, you take charge of him.

HONORIUS: Gladly, gladly.

(aside) Ah, this is hell.

IMPERIA: Here I am for this solemn audience!

LEONE: Enter, my dear guests.

(a crowd of creditors, including Shylock, enters)

Come in without trepidation and greet our queen of everything. Madame, I present to you my best friends, honest folk who dress me, outfit me, furnish me, barber me, shoe me and nourish me. They are, for the most part, fathers of families, and their virtues can be read in their faces. They are not all gentlemen, but they deserve to be, for it is thanks to them that we maintain our place worthily. Happy the land that is able to offer the world such citizens!

(pointing to Shylock) I particularly present to you Messire Shylock, the patriarch of loaners.

SHYLOCK: Leave me alone, Marquis. I will present myself well enough.

UBALDO: (low to Leone) That one is not drunk.

SHYLOCK: (to Imperia) I salute you, my sister?

IMPERIA: What do you mean?

SHYLOCK: Yes, my sister.

IMPERIA: But—.

SHYLOCK: I am Usury, you are Luxury. Venice belongs to both of us. Misfortune to those imprudent enough to cross our door.

IMPERIA: (aside) Strange old geezer!

LEONE: Beware of your heart, Imperia. Shylock is dangerous!

SHYLOCK: Ah, ah! The Marquis Leone is so gay. That's what youth is!

LEONE: (to Ubaldo) You see quite well he's softened up.

SHYLOCK: (aside) Honorius is here, that's well.

LEONE: (to Creditors) Now, my dear guests, would you like to try to win some florins? These fine ladies will assist you at the tournament. You consent! Bravo!

AZZOLI: (to Ubaldo) They are charming.

UBALDO: (low) To despoiling the creditors!

AZZOLI: To the pillage!

(All the tables are crowded)

HONORIUS: (aside) Let's do it!

(aloud to Shylock) Good evening, Jew.

SHYLOCK: (bowing) My young master.

HONORIUS: What were you saying to La Signora?

SHYLOCK: I was enticing her to come see some jewels I've purchased.

HONORIUS: Stolen, rather.

SHYLOCK: As you like, my young master. I no longer argue with my clients.

HONORIUS: Well, we are going to see them, and if they suit her, I will make the acquisition.

IMPERIA: Truly?

HONORIUS: Didn't I swear?

SHYLOCK: How fine it is to be generous!

HONORIUS: Would you like to play with me?

SHYLOCK: Oh, I understand nothing about that.

HONORIUS: What's that matter? It's luck.

LEONE: (at the back) You lost. Your revenge? Another loss. You don't have much luck right now.

SHYLOCK: (meaningfully) Ah, it's chance.

HONORIUS: My God, yes.

SHYLOCK: And how does one seize it, I beg you?

HONORIUS: You shake the horn, throw the dice, count the points, and whoever has the most wins the round.

SHYLOCK: Nothing more simple nor more ingenious.

HONORIUS: Try it.

SHYLOCK: I'll seem so clumsy.

HONORIUS: Not at all.

SHYLOCK: Since you wish it.

(going to a table)

IMPERIA: (to Honorius) I'm going to place myself near you to bring you luck.

(lowering her voice) Are you sure of your dice?

HONORIUS: Huh?

IMPERIA: (offering him others) Take these, my dear.

HONORIOUS: Infamy.

IMPERIA: Against a Jew?

HONORIUS: (pushing her away) Never!

IMPERIA: After all, it's your business!

SHYLOCK: (aside) Still some minutes to wait.

HONORIUS: Well?

SHYLOCK: I'm at your orders, my young master.

HONORIUS: What are we playing?

SHYLOCK: Why—.

HONORIUS: One hundred ducats?

SHYLOCK: Oh, that's quite little. Let's play for what you owe me.

HONORIUS: Two thousand ducats?

SHYLOCK: Yes.

HONORIUS: I consent to it. For a single throw?

SHYLOCK: For a single throw.

HONORIUS: Double or nothing then.

SHYLOCK: Not at all. I need another wager.

IMPERIA: What's that?

SHYLOCK: His life!

IMPERIA: What are you saying?

SHYLOCK: His life! Only, Signora, we won't use your dice.

IMPERIA: See here, gentlemen. This crazy Shylock is demanding that Honorius stake his life against two thousand ducats.

SHYLOCK: What's so bizarre about that proposition? No one is forced to accept it, but I have the right to ask it. I'm in business and I try not to sell except to persons who are solvent; if I wager you money, I won't be paid, consequently, I've made a fool's bargain. I am, therefore, constrained to demand a positive pledge from you, a palpable one, which suits me better than others. To be sure, my manner of acting is not strictly equitable, and the friend of Signor Honorius, the ship owner Andronicus, who is the most just of the just, could himself find nothing against it.

Remark, also, that the worst luck is mine, since from my point of view as a merchant and an accountant, I am playing a sum against zero! Indeed, that's the way it is. Luck, which decides these games. I might, it's true, see a Christian die, but I might also lose my money, and you know the cursed Jews prefer money to all else. Admit that this is all perfectly logical.

LEONE: Is this finished?

SHYLOCK: Not yet; if you'll allow, I am trying to convince you I'm right.

LEONE: Continue. We will have our turn.

SHYLOCK: I was saying that each has the right to understand and do business in his own fashion. Lord Andronicus, who possesses a great reputation for honor and probity has the simplicity to loan money gratis, and he wants to reduce usury in Venice. I dispose my wealth otherwise, I do not have sterile sheep in my sheepfold, and I make my ducats multiply in the fastest and best way possible. In good conscience is it I who am wrong or is it Signor Andronicus?

HONORIUS: Andronicus will end by ruining you and driving you from Venice.

SHYLOCK: Who lives will see, my young master, who lives will see.

(pointing to creditors) Look a bit at those poor devils who also pride themselves on commerce. All the same, I observe to you, here's not one Jew among them. They have stupidly allowed themselves to lose to you, but if they proposed the same wager that I do, they would still be your creditors, they would have the same right that I have, that of putting you in prison for your debts.

ALL: In prison?

SHYLOCK: Yes.

HONORIUS: Insolent!

LEONE: Let me speak to him. Shylock and I, gentlemen, are old acquaintances.

SHYLOCK: Indeed.

LEONE: Have you the memory of it?

SHYLOCK: Much.

LEONE: You recollect being cudgeled by this hand?

SHYLOCK: I recall it perfectly, although long years have wrinkled my face, whitened my hair and dried up my heart! After having struck me you returned with an officer of the police and you found me mad with sorrow between a cadaver and an empty cradle! I begged you, yes, I begged you to return my child. A word from you would have left me free, you kept silent; I think you even laughed. Thy tied my hands and threw me in a dungeon where I remained for two years.

LEONE: If you don't leave instantly, I promise you the same correction and the same dungeon.

SHYLOCK: I won't leave.

LEONE: But—

SHYLOCK: I won't leave.

LEONE: Take care!

SHYLOCK: I fear nothing.

LEONE: For the last time!

SHYLOCK: O my fine patricians, the time for violence and good pleasure is over. The new Doge who is, I admit, an honest man has said, rightfully, that Venice is a Republic of merchants above all, that we merchants have become a powerful force and that he had an interest in taking care of us. Thanks to him the law protects us as much as Christians, and it's no longer permitted to fail in engagements that one takes *vis-à-vis* us. The strictness of the Doge is inflexible with regard to commercial transactions, and the signature of the debtor is no longer an idle title in the hand of a creditor. A man is going to leave this palace to go to prison; but that man is not me. Signor Honorius, my two thousand ducats, if you please.

HONORIUS: Wait till tomorrow.

SHYLOCK: You cannot pay them on the spot?

HONORIUS: No, but—

IMPERIA: (aside) Decidedly, he's ruined!

SHYLOCK: Then say your goodbyes to your mistress, you'll end this brilliant night behind bars.

LEONE: Oh, we won't suffer it.

ALL: No, no—

SHYLOCK: Take care in your turn, I hear bailiffs.

HONORIUS: Do you hate me?

SHYLOCK: Yes.

HONORIUS: Why?

SHYLOCK: Because you are the friend of Andronicus who ruins my business; because there is no longer any happiness for me, the happiness of others is intolerable! But what are these police doing?

(going toward the door) This way, this way.

(he finds himself face to face with Andronicus)

ALL: Andronicus!

SHYLOCK: (aside) Him, again!

ANDRONICUS: Jew, here's your money

(to Honorius) You are free.

HONORIUS: My friend!

SHYLOCK: First of all, let me count the sum. Good values, good values, excellent values. I might exact the reimbursement in specie, but I am content with this paper. I really like paper, there are so many signatures on it. You have a very generous friend in Signor Andronicus but I fear he won't get rich in this profession.

ANDRONICUS: (to Honorius) How much did he loan you?

HONORIUS: A thousand ducats.

ANDRONICUS: And he gets back two thousand. Shylock, you are the most ignoble of usurers.

SHYLOCK: I am what I am, my young colleague.

ANDRONICUS: Don't give that name to one who scorns you.

SHYLOCK: Scorn? A soap bubble, a big empty word that is abused. Scorn is to hate as vanity is to pride. Besides, do you know me to judge me? Wait till you grow a little more beard on your chin, young man.

(aside) Oh, this is the one I'd like to get hold of.

ANDRONICUS: Poor old geezer, your impotent rage makes me pity you.

LEONE: You are too indulgent, sir. The insolence of this Jew has become scandalous, and it's no longer to the magistrates we shall plead, it's to the Doge himself.

ANDRONICUS: You might do it as of tomorrow, Marquis Leone, because all the nobility of Venice is being convoked at the Ducal Palace.

LEONE: Do you know why?

ANDRONICUS: They are talking of important news that the Doge has received from the fleet and the army.

LEONE: Some disaster, perhaps?

SHYLOCK: In that case, they'll have need of me.

ANDRONICUS: Let's leave, Honorius.

INPERIA: (to Honorius) You are leaving me?

HONORIUS: (pointing her out to Andronicus) She's the one.

ANDRONICUS: (coldly) Ah!

(to Imperia) You love him, Madame?

IMPERIA: Yes, I love him.

ANDRONICUS: And you didn't cast the diamonds with which you are covered at the Jew's feet? To ransom Honorius, you didn't even detach one of the pearls he gave you?

HONORIUS: (aside) It's true!

ANDRONICUS: Let's leave, I tell you.

HONORIUS: (aside) O cowardly heart!

(moving away, dragged by Andronicus)

IMPERIA: He'll come back, if I want him.

SHYLOCK: (low to Imperia) My beautiful lady, I have magnificent stones. Come see them.

IMPERIA: I will go.

LEONE: (to Shylock) Will you leave now?

ALL: Begone, Jew, begone.

SHYLOCK: Till tomorrow, Milords at the palace of the Doge.

CURTAIN

ACT II

The Palace of the Doge.

ANDRONICUS: We have a few minutes before the audience with the Doge?

USHER: Yes, milord.

(he leaves)

ANDRONICUS: Honorius, you must forget that woman; you must renounce this life of dissipation and idleness.

HONORIUS: I will try, my friend, but I cannot answer for myself.

ANDRONICUS: Such weakness is unworthy of a man.

HONORIUS: I know it, but I've never been able to conquer it. I've told myself a thousand times that these loves are false, and that these kisses kill; in nights of orgy, a cloud passes for a moment before my eyes, a sepulchral vapor envelops the crystal, the decorations, the lights and the laughter of Bacchantes, no longer for me is anything but lugubrious riots. Then suddenly, I feel the clear and cold look of Imperia penetrate my heart, the cloud disappears, the feast lights back up, sparkling, and I deliver myself without remorse to all the fury of pleasure.

ANDRONICUS: Still, since yesterday, the prestige which surrounded your mistress must have vanished; she would have let you be imprisoned without offering an obole, without shedding a tear.

HONORIUS: Yes. It's sad to think about.

ANDRONICUS: You gone, the fest would have continued and your place would have been taken by another.

HONORIUS: I've never believed that Imperia had a heart.

ANDRONICUS: Well!

HONORIUS: If I told you despite this I thought I was loved by her—?

ANDRONI: Ah, that's craziness!

HONORIUS: You see where I am at, my dear Andronicus, and you dream of curing me? Heavens, at this moment I feel she's looking at me through space. Oh, I am not deceiving myself! Truly, there are some moments in which I pity you, extinguishing your youth in work and austerity, unaware of evil, and not gnawing as we do at these beautiful fruits of perdition! The first time I saw Imperia I was sort of dazzled; as for you, you look at her with the eyes of a dead man. What man are you, really?

ANDRONICUS: A poor creature consumed by sadness who doubts happiness and is attached to life only through duty. In Smyrna I had a friend, in Venice, I no longer have one; my heart is in a monastery where I walk alone.

HONORIUS: Can you imagine that I don't love you?

ANDRONICUS: Do you think sometimes of Smyrna, our childhood, our games?

HONORIUS: Oh, often!

ANDRONICUS: Well, brother, I have the presentiment that horrible misfortunes threaten both of us here. Let's return to our old country.

HONORIUS: Let's leave quickly then. Let's leave before Imperia calls me back.

ANDRONICUS: (aside) No woman will keep me.

(aloud) As soon as the audience with the Doge is over we'll make our preparations.

HONORIUS: Praise God! You've got a great idea there! Now how I breathe from afar the natal air, I feel myself full of good will. You will teach me business, you will give me a ship to command. I am going to become a model of economy, and all fathers will want me for a son-in-law.

ANDRONICUS: Your dear gayety reminds me of beautiful times.

HONORIUS: You are leaving Venice like this? And there I was thinking you amorous! My wise friend, I ask your pardon for having slandered you.

ANDRONICUS: (aside) O mad passion, die without confidant or witnesses; dig yourself an unknown tomb in my heart. It's decided; I'm going to see her for the last time.

HONORIUS: (aside) What's Imperia going to say?

(Enter Leone, Ubaldo, Azzoli)

LEONE: It's scandalous, it's intolerable. The Ducal palace has become a public bazaar. Everyone comes in, like Noah's ark, even animals.

AZZOLI: And the Israeli bucks smell strong!

LEONE: I just bumped in to His Highness Shylock on the Lion stairs.

UBALDO: There's more Jewry here than in a full synagogue!

LEONE: The day on which the nobility is convoked is an act intended to humiliate the patricians. The Doge had better look to it.

UBALDO: What the Devil does he want of us?

LEONE: Don't you see that the poor man is at the end of his government and he's decided to consult us about affairs of state?

UBALDO: Right! Is that something that concerns us?

LEONE: We are going to be enlightened, because here's the Doge leaving the chapel with his daughter.

UBALDO: Is she still pretty, his daughter?

LEONE: As for me, I find her charming.

AZZOLI: Oh, don't speak to me of these cold beauties.

ANDRONICUS: (aside) May God take my life and add it to hers.

(Enter the Doge and Ginerva with their suite.)

DOGE: (to Patricians) I greet you, milords. I desired to see you by us and near us to address your vows to heaven for our glorious Republic, but still you are welcome.

(lowering his voice) Go back inside, Ginerva, drive from

your face those villainous clouds, and amongst your companions, forget the austere old geezer who loves you, the cares and worries of power are not made for you! The misfortune of Venice is great, but God will protect us. Your prayers have disarmed Him.

GINERVA: I've profited from your lessons, father, and I intend to render myself worthy of serious times; let my country exact all sacrifices from me, I am ready to make them; its prosperity is more dear to me than life, and its glory is my dream.

(she leaves)

ANDRONICUS: (aside) Chance did not lead her eyes in my direction; luckier is the beggar at whom she at least looks while giving him alms.

DOGE: Let me be left alone with my patricians.

(to Andronicus) Don't stray far my young friend. I may perhaps have need of you.

ANDRONICUS: I am at your Lordship's orders.

LEONE: (low to Honorius) Go console Imperia. The wretched woman is horribly sad.

HONORIUS: The Marquis is jesting?

UBALDO: No, I swear to you, she refused a delightful

ride in a gondola this morning.

HONORIUS: (aside) I haven't yet left for Smyrna!

(he follows Andronicus)

DOGE: Noble lords, a double disaster has just struck Venice! Our fleet has lost a dozen vessels, and twenty galleys in the Black Sea; our army has been destroyed by the Dalmatians beneath the walls of Zara. In this extremity, I must address myself to you, first of all. To act otherwise would be to insult you. For my part, I ask no other honor than to offer the Republic all the ducats and precious objects I have.

AZZOLI: (aside) There we go!

DOGE: (to Leone) Your turn, Marquis.

LEONE: My purse at this moment resembles the coffers of the state. It is empty.

DOGE: There was a century when Venice was at war with Genoa, one of your ancestors, Count Aldo, broke up all his vessels.

LEONE: I still owe mine.

(he bows and moves away)

DOGE: (to Ubaldo) Yours. Our historians glorify your ancestor who, after ruining himself for Venice went to die in the Holy Land.

UBALDO: I've lost a lot. I've been forced to engage all my wealth.

(moving away like Leone)

DOGE: (to Azzoli) Your turn. In the last attack against Palermo, a patrician fitted out six vessels at her own expense. That was your aunt.

AZZOLI: May your lordship make me heirs of my six uncles and I will imitate my aunt.

(he moves away, too)

DOGE: (aside) Come on, poor Venice, there's nothing here for you. Pass on your way, poor beggar.

LEONE: Your Lordship will allow me to demand justice.

DOGE: Against whom?

LEONE: Against the Jews whose insolence—

DOGE: But that's ingratitude on your part, for they are the ones who make you live. Ah, still, I understand your noble indignation; the pagans. no question, don't wish to loan any more, so kick them out and let them be despoiled very rapidly! Thus to miscreants.

UBALDO: Your words are harsh.

DOGE: As for your anger, I am far from sharing it; the Jews are peaceful subjects, devoted completely to commerce, incapable of exciting any disorder, they respect the laws and they will be protected by them.

LEONE: In that case we'll avenge ourselves, by ourselves!

DOGE: I don't advise you to do that.

(The Patricians withdraw to the side)

LEONE: Decidedly, he's conspiring against the nobility.

UBALDO: He's been won over by Shylock.

LEONE: There must be an accusation against him!

DOGE: (dismissing them with a gesture) May God keep you.

(they leave)

There's not one worthy of the name of citizen. But at any cost, I must find money or Venice is lost.

(aloud) Show Lord Andronicus in.

(Andronicus is shown in)

How pale you are, Andronicus. You seem troubled. Is something wrong?

ANDRONICUS: Oh, nothing, Milord. Some bad news I've just received.

(aside) The first reversal.

(aloud) What does your Lordship wish?

DOGE: The Republic needs to borrow a considerable sum, and I hope that with the concurrence of Christian merchants you can loan it to her.

ANDRONICUS: Ah, it's now especially, that I understand the complete extent of my misfortune, because Venice is a second country for me and I would have been happy to come to her aid, but read this, Milord, read.

(he delivers a paper to him)

DOGE: (after having read it) Two boats coming from Tripoli and loaded with the most precious wares have perished. That's an immense loss!

ANDRONICUS: Half of my fortune. Oh, if the rest could suffice, I would confide it without regret to your noble hands, but for me to raise a large sum I would need the support of my colleagues; but the news of this disaster is already known in the Rialto; it must bring a terrible blow to my credit, and by charging myself with the interests of

Venice, I would compromise them rather than serve them.

DOGE: Ah! Times are bad and God tests us all.

(aside) Let's try a last resort.

(aloud) Find the Jew Shylock and bring him to me.

(to Andronicus) The dangers of Venice worry me cruelly, but I take no less a very sympathetic share of your misfortune, and the esteem I have for you has just increased. Hearts like yours are so rare!

ANDRONICUS: Oh, if he knew.

(going to leave) Milord.

DOGE: Stay, Andronicus, stay as a friend and as a counselor of the Doge.

SHYLOCK: (entering, aside) It's always me they turn to.

(aloud) Here I am ready to obey you, venerable Doge.

(to Andronicus) Plague, my young master, there's a rumor about you in the Rialto. Ah, it's a great loss, but you are rich, so rich! No doubt, it's last month's tempest which swallowed your two ships. Exactly. I was thinking of you last night, and I congratulated myself on not having made too large a commerce. This cursed sea so quickly drowns the opulence and lives of men. Courage, I said, courage, storm soothe the waves, break the sails, hide the reefs extinguish the light house! As for me, I have nothing to fear in my poor shops and making all those reflections, I rubbed my hands!

DOGE: You are bad!

SHYLOCK: I have no son. Why should I be good?

DOGE: It's not we who caused your misfortune.

SHYLOCK: You haven't punished the assassins?

DOGE: I've vainly tried to discover them.

SHYLOCK: Oh, I'm not reproaching you. One would have avenged the child of a Christian.

DOGE: You are slandering me. The scales I hold are equal for all.

SHYLOCK: In the end I'm not arguing. I have my idea.

DOGE: Shylock, it's necessary that you count me one hundred thousand silver marks.

SHYLOCK: God of Abraham!

DOGE: I need them before tomorrow.

SHYLOCK: One hundred thousand silver marks! Why,

break down the doors of my shop, pillage my safe, sell my merchandise, make us drag to market ourselves, and all of that won't produce a thousand marks.

DOGE: Are you speaking the truth?

SHYLOCK Faith of—

ANDRONICUS: (interrupting him) He's going to lie. The Jews of Venice possess ten times the sum you are demanding.

SHYLOCK: Why's this man meddling in it? If he remains here I won't speak.

DOGE: I beg him to remain, and I order you to reply.

SHYLOCK: Still violence.

DOGE: What violence are you talking about?

ANDRONICUS: He doesn't believe it.

SHYLOCK: Let them come to seek in Venice justice and good faith. In the end you are the stronger, tyrannizing us, as in Germany, persecuting us as in France.

DOGE: So then, you are refusing to loan the Republic one hundred thousand silver marks.

SHYLOCK: Loan! Your Lordship said loan?

DOGE: Yes.

SHYLOCK: It's not a forced tax but a loan?

DOGE: Certainly.

SHYLOCK: Have you good guarantees?

DOGE: Such as Venice always gives.

SHYLOCK: A loan. Ah, that's a different matter.

DOGE: Well?

SHYLOCK: I do not despair that by making sacrifices we might succeed in raising a quarter of that sum, in question. Yes, really a quarter.

DOGE: Not more?

SHYLOCK: Half, perhaps.

DOGE: I need it all.

SHYLOCK: If we began by discussing conditions?

DOGE: What are you demanding?

SHYLOCK: I demand, for myself and my associates, as reimbursement and interest, the revenues from Constantinople and Candia: for two years.

DOGE: Why, the revenues from Candia alone are worth four times that sum.

SHYLOCK: I'm well aware of that.

DOGE: That's exorbitant.

SHYLOCK: I'm not forcing you.

ANDRONICUS: Vile usurer!

SHYLOCK: Loan the money yourself, man of integrity, give to the world a new example of your disinterest and your generosity. Save the Republic! One hundred thousand marks, if you please? The means of not loaning them when one has them? Why, you do not have them otherwise, I wouldn't be here? Shylock is indeed only a last resort. One has recourse to his purse only because one has found others empty. So, because Shylock is not a ninny, he pulls the purse strings, and he does the right thing.

DOGE: You are odiously abusing your position.

SHYLOCK: Not the least in the world. I am profiting by it. This is a business matter, and each seeks his advantage. Just as you try to diminish your loss I am trying to increase my gain, and we are both within our rights. But once again, I am not forcing anyone. I have nothing to loan you.

ANDRONICUS: (low to Doge) Your Lordship cannot

submit to such conditions.

DOGE: (low) Pity me, Andronicus.

(aloud to Shylock) I will transfer to you for two years the revenues from Candia and Constantinople, if you pay me cash tomorrow.

SHYLOCK: Pardon, I am still asking for something. A trifle, assuredly. My most rich colleagues, those who I would need most for this loan are almost all jewelers, and as I know them to be amateurs in precious jewels, your Lordship will give them a gift of useless jewel boxes that are used only in days of solemnity.

DOGE: They can have them with the exception of my Ducal ring.

(with effort) Isn't that enough?

SHYLOCK: Yes, if you include your daughter's jewels.

ANDRONICUS: This is infamous!

DOGE: Yes, infamous!

SHYLOCK: Don't get carried away, Milord. The deal fails, that's all.

GINERVA: It's concluded. Shylock, take this box and God save Venice!

DOGE: Ginerva!

SHYLOCK: That's fine, Miss, that's very fine!

ANDRONICUS: (to Shylock) You don't have the audacity.

GINERVA: Let him alone, Lord Andronicus.

ANDRONICUS: (aside) She knows my name!

GINERVA: This old man has suffered and misfortune has made him inflexible. He's to be pitied. Shylock, I've often prayed God for you, and I've asked him in tears that he return your child to you. Shylock, I am only a woman! You've taken the bad way; you are unjust to treat us all as accomplices in a crime of some unknown rogues. To pardon is better than to punish, and vengeance is horrible especially when the one who is taking vengeance has white hair!

ANDRONICUS: (low to Shylock) Doesn't her sweet voice disarm you?

SHYLOCK: My son would have love, too, but they killed him on me.

(aloud) What's in this box?

GINERVA: All the jewelry I possess.

SHYLOCK: All?

GINERVA: Yes.

SHYLOCK: Less the necklace you are wearing.

DOGE: Ah, that's too much.

GINERVA: Let me speak to him.

(to Shylock) This necklace has no value

SHYLOCK: I beg your pardon, Miss, the diamonds are of very fine water.

GINERVA: My mother hung them on my neck when she was dying, and it never leaves me. I keep them like a sacred relic.

SHYLOCK: I understand that. Keep them then.

GINERVA: Oh, thanks!

SHYLOCK: Only I won't loan the hundred thousand marks.

DOGE: Ah, this is debasing, and ignominious! Leave or I'll have you driven out with switches.

GINERVA: Father!

ANDRONICUS: It's still a punishment too gentle for him.

GINERVA: Lord Andronicus!

SHYLOCK: I'm withdrawing, but the Republic is lost.

GINERVA: And if I give you this necklace, you will loan the money?

SHYLOCK: Yes. I have only one word.

GINERVA: Here it is!

DOGE: I won't allow it.

GINERVA: It belongs to me, father. And I am giving it to Venice. Dear necklace, let me pass you one last time to my lips. O holy woman, you who from the heights of heaven see our anguish, forgive me. One more kiss, one more goodbye. My heart is torn apart.

(to Shylock) Take it, take it!

SHYLOCK: Magnificent diamonds.

ANDRONICUS: (aside) Oh, to see her weep.

(low to Shylock) I must speak to you; I will go to your place tonight.

SHYLOCK: That's too great an honor for a Jew. I will

wait on you, my master, I will wait on you.

(aside) This time, I've got him.

(aloud) Tomorrow, at daybreak, I will bring the Doge one hundred thousand marks.

DOGE: You horrify me; get out.

ANDRONICUS: (aside) Ginerva, I'll get your necklace for you.

CURTAIN

ACT III

The child's room in Shylock's house. Door at back. At the right of the door a cradle. In the middle of the stage a table around which are arranged Shylock and the Jews.

SHYLOCK: So, it's agreed. I will furnish a third of the sum and you will combine to complete the rest. The profits will be received pro rata in accord with what each of us have advanced. As for these jewels, you can share them as of the present, or rather, no, I need to be alone. Take the box to Jacob's place and as you will be arguing, if it's possible shut yourselves in a cellar so as not to give a scandal by your quarrels to Christians who will pass by the house.

JACOB: And you, Shylock, have you chosen your share?

SHYLOCK: I'm only keeping this necklace. You don't find me too demanding.

JACOB: No, surely.

SHYLOCK: Tell me, Jacob, do you concern yourself with astrology?

JACOB: A little bit, master.

SHYLOCK: The weather is favorable to navigation?

JACOB: There have been these last months many disasters, principally in the Southern Ocean, and towards the Cape of Storms.

SHYLOCK: Ah!

JACOB: I am rarely mistaken.

SHYLOCK: You also are one of the best informed in the Rialto. Do you know from what country Andronicus is expecting his new ships?

JACOB: From the Indies.

SHYLOCK: In that case, they will pass the Cape of Storms. Mighty fine! I thank you.

(to Jews) Go, my brothers, and be especially careful the money is here at daybreak. The Doge will be counting the minutes until my arrival.

JACOB: May the God of Moses protect you.

SHYLOCK: One more time, go into a cellar to share things.

(All the Jews leave)

SHYLOCK: (alone) Today is the anniversary of the crime! Twenty years have elapsed since that horrible moment and I haven't yet shocked the world with my vengeance. Twenty years! And Christians proclaim me the most ferocious and pitiless of men! What have I done to deserve that name? Nothing yet. I am a lamb, a veritable lamb. I've practiced usury with sensuality; thousands of the best families have been ruined by me. From time to time I send a patrician to rot on prison straw for debts, and I'm on my way to pushing Venice into the abyss. Trifles, all that! The most vulgar hater would have done the same. Still, I've done nothing yet! Also, the voice of my child is screaming to me for justice every night and the blood of my poor Sarah, which splashed on these flagstones, reminds me each day of my duty. Pardon me this slowness, my dear shades! But it's also true, in all this human multitude, up to now, I haven't found a single victim who was worthy of being sacrificed to you. One doesn't furiously pursue enemies such as Ubaldo and Leone, one crushes them and moves on. The Executioner will waste his time torturing these folks because vice has already killed them. Fine pleasure that, to chop up their cadavers. Speak to me of living and warm flesh which palpitates and bleeds under the knife. Great. A noise of steps. No question it's Andronicus. This young man is handsome, honest, generous and devoted. He knows friendship, he aspires to love. Still, he's too many on this earth. Such phenomena are a bad example to humanity. Andronicus, if my foresight is just and my calculations certain, you are striding at this moment towards your tomb. Before knowing you, vengeance for me was only a habit, thanks to you it's becoming a pleasure. Your decree is to be found in this thought which emerges from my mouth with a sob. My son would have been this age! And you will live when he is dead, and you will be happy while I suffer? No, no! The blood stain is becoming moist like a miracle! You can enter, mad fly, the old spider has spread his web.

ANDRONICUS: Good evening, Shylock.

SHYLOCK: Milord is right on time. What can I do to serve, Milord?

ANDRONICUS: A lot.

SHYLOCK: A sickly creature like me? You astonish me.

ANDRONICUS: I'm going straight to the point. Would you sell me that necklace that you have?

SHYLOCK: No, lord, I'm keeping it.

ANDRONICUS: Come on, will you?

SHYLOCK: What do you want? Old geezers have these fantasies. Recall the determination I had to get it.

ANDRONICUS: To get profit out of it.

SHYLOCK: Not at all. For the love of art.

ANDRONICUS: Still, I need it.

SHYLOCK: Impossible.

ANDRONICUS: I must have it.

SHYLOCK: I'm quite calm. You won't steal it from me.

ANDRONICUS: Look, Jew, your tricks are useless. I'm not coming here to bargain.

SHYLOCK: Ah, but since I don't wish to sell.

ANDRONICUS: I will give you the price you ask, whatever it may be.

SHYLOCK: I doubt it.

ANDRONICUS: Try.

SHYLOCK: I repeat to you I really want to keep this necklace very much.

ANDRONICUS: State your price.

SHYLOCK: If I decide to sell it, it will be, I admit to you, only for an enormous price.

ANDRONICUS: How much are you asking?

HYLOCK: You will be shocked.

ANDRONICUS: From you, I expect anything.

SHYLOCK: You would be committing a folly.

ANDRONICUS: What do you care? Come on, speak.

SHYLOCK: I want sixty thousand sequins for it.

ANDRONICUS: I'm buying it.

AHYLOCK: Marvelous. No hesitation.

ANDRONICUS: Get me something to write on.

SHYLOCK: Gladly. Ah, the Signora will be glad to get this necklace back.

ANDRONICUS: (aside) Blessed be ruin and misery if I spare her some tears!

(aloud) How much delay do you grant me to pay you?

SHYLOCK: A delay? But I want cash.

ANDRONICUS: It would be better to say you don't want to sell. The means of raising a sum so great?

SHYLOCK: You have so much credit in the Venetian market. And yet, since the loss of your vessels, whatever the case may be, I still find you good. And I shall content myself with your note. The term of one month will be enough for you?

ANDRONICUS: Yes.

(aside) I am expecting my ship from India from one day to the next.

(aloud) I'm going to write my obligation.

SHYLOCK: Excuse me; it's my custom to dictate these things myself. I'm a bit maniacal in the matter of commercial formulas.

ANDRONI: I'm waiting.

SHYLOCK: (dictating) I, Andronicus, merchant, native of Smyrna and living in Venice take the formal and absolute engagement to pay to the Jew Shylock, a month from today's date, the sum of sixty thousand sequins as the price for a necklace he's sold and delivered to me.

ANDRONICUS: Right. I'll put in the date and sign it.

SHYLOCKL Oh, not yet. Youth is in such a hurry. Are you counting to pay me on some return?

ANDRONICUS: On rich merchandise en route to Venice.

SHYLOCK: Over land?

ANDRONICUS: No.

SHYLOCK: So much the worse. The waves are so treacherous.

ANDRONICUS: Do you imagine that all my ships must fatally perish?

SHYLOCK: I don't say that, but still, it possibly could happen and what would I do if such a misfortune occurred.

ANDRONICUS: You would have the recourse that the law gives you.

SHYLOCK: Oh, that's nothing. Satan loses his rights and prison won't make you find the money.

ANDRONICUS: Once more, your fears are chimeras.

SHYLOCK: All the same, you won't have the necklace if you don't give me more positive guarantees.

ANDRONICUS: Such as?

SHYLOCK: Write.

ANDRONICUS: Tell me your conditions first.

SHYLOCK: What's the good of that? If they are repugnant you are still free to tear up the note.

ANDRONICUS: So be it,

SHYLOCK: (dictating) If I do not effect payment on the

day prescribed, I authorize the Jew Shylock to cut off from my breast a pound of flesh.

ANDRONICUS: Horror!

SHYLOCK: Look carefully at these Christians! They make notes so as not to pay them. They resign themselves gladly to dishonor. But if one demands a single drop of blood from them, to answer for their debt, they shrivel their white hand and throw away their pen in a cowardly manner.

ANDRONICUS: Jew—

SHYLOCK: It's the way I said,

ANDRONICUS: What infernal thought have you got then?

SHYLOCK: Me? That I keep this necklace. Ah, your devotion is not valorous. It recoils before the least peril, and even before an imaginary peril.

ANDRONICUS: You don't maintain this horrible condition?

SHYLOCK: Rather than renounce it, I would have myself cut to pieces!

(pointing to the necklace) Here it is, the holy relic that a dying mother hung about the neck of her daughter! Each of these diamonds is worth a man's life and Signor Andronicus doesn't want to risk a drop of his blood for the whole thing. Well, by Abraham. I want to be generous for once. I will tell the story to the daughter of the Doge. I will return her the necklace without exacting an obole, and I consent to be roasted alive if her charming lips do not press my old wrinkled hands. Goodbye, Lord Andronicus, goodbye.

ANDRONICUS: Satan! I signed it!

SHYLOCK: Right, I find you.

(takes the note and delivers the necklace) Give it to me, give it to me.

ANDRONICUS: You hate me, Shylock! You've set a sinister trap for me. But my God will protect me against you.

SHYLOCK: I hate you, I set a trap for you? Why not believe instead that I am rendering you a service and that this terrible clause is only a whim of a sick old man. In any case, you have a simple way to annul it, that's by paying me exactly.

ANDRONICUS: You will be!

SHYLOCK: I'm counting on it, because I really want those sixty-thousand sequins.

ANDRONICUS: (aside) Ginerva! Ginerva!

(aloud) Sum complete, thanks.

SHYLOCK: Didn't I say I was rendering you a service? This has certainty; still, I wouldn't have made this bargain with anyone but you. If by chance you are deceiving yourself on my account?

ANDRONICUS: Oh, no! As treacherous and veiled as is your glance, I read mortal hate in it, but I defy you.

SHYLOCK: (aside) Feather-brain.

(aloud) In a month, milord.

ANDRONICUS: In a month.

(he leaves)

SHYLOCK: Oh, the good note the excellent note. Let Andronicus pay or not, I am certain of winning. But if he doesn't pay in silver, it's impossible. Where will he find the money? I'm going to bring the last blow to his credit, and trace a circle of suspicion around him. As for his fragile ships, I commend them to the storms. Storms are intelligent. Oh, I am a clever man. I know life! Still, let's put this admirable note in a safe place.

(Shylock leaves by a side door. Honorius and Imperia enter from the rear.)

HONORIUS: Where are you leading me, dear beauty?

IMPERIA: We've arrived.

HONORIUS: God damn me, it's Shylock's house.

IMPERIA: Yes.

HONORIUS: What are we coming to do in this lair?

IMPERIA: You've forgotten?

HONORIUS: What

IMPERIA: The jewels he must show me. And your oath to do the impossible to satisfy my fantasy?

HONORIUS: I renew it.

IMPERIA: See that you do.

SHYLOCK: (returning, aside) Ah, this courtesan. I'd forgotten her.

IMPERIA: Master Shylock, we've come to see your marvels.

SHYLOCK: Have you set your desire on some jewel? You need a diadem, a clasp, earrings?

IMPERIA: I need a necklace.

(to Honorius) Right?

HONORIUS: Certainly.

SHYLOCK: A necklace. Ah, I had a magnificent one just now, but I sold it.

IMPERIA: Sold it! That's the one I want.

(to Shylock) Where'd you get it?

SHYLOCK: From the daughter of the Doge.

IMPERIA: From that beautiful and virtuous Ginerva. One reason the more that I must have it.

HONORIUS: (to Shylock) Old clumsy! Why didn't you wait for me?

IMPERIA: Don't get carried away against him, my dear. When one is amorous of a woman and that woman has a caprice, one doesn't rebuke oneself so quickly. I pass with you before the shop of a gold smith, I notice an object, you pay for it, I take it away. That's a vulgar gallantry. But to-day, it doesn't suffice to pull some florins from one's pocket. It's almost a question of a conquest. Honorius, I intend to have that necklace.

HONORIUS: You shall have it!

SHYLOCK: (aside) Ha, ha—

IMPERIA: What are you going to do?

HONORIUS: Nothing more simple, by Jove. I am going to offer the buyer whatever he wants for it.

IMPERIA: Oh, I hope better. I suppose that the unknown possessor has a capricious mistress, who wants this gift, and you will be obliged to cut his throat.

HONORIUS: He can count on that at need.

(to Shylock) The name of this character?

SHYLOCK: Andronicus!

HONORIUS: Him!

IMPERIA: Mercy! It's a failed affair! The magnanimous Andronicus will deliver the necklace to you with enthusiasm.

SHYLOCK: I doubt it.

HONORIUS: Why?

SHYLOCK: Because he paid very dearly for it and seemed intent on keeping it.

IMPERIA: Bravo! The romance is getting complicated and I feel more excited by the game. When will you go to your friend?

HONORIUS: Why—

IMPERIA: That hesitation is insulting. The rest of us, we have our pride. To return with empty hands is to renounce me forever.

HONORIUS: I will do my duty, Madame.

IMPERIA: Oh. What a solemn tone. Let's have enough wit, at least, not to get angry with each other in advance, and come sup with me. You will take the time necessary to plan your formidable expedition.

SHYLOCK: (low to Imperia) You won't have the necklace.

IMPERIA: You will see it tomorrow on the neck of my chamber maid.

SHYLOCK: (aside) The love of these women is hate.

(Imperia leaves with Honorius)

Now there's a man who's ready to commit an evil dead!

(silence)

Fraternal friendship of these two young men, a flame pure and sacred, you'll snuff it out like this poor lamp, and now let's begin our night, the same that twenty years ago,— horrible, horrible— It's the hour when the empty cradle rocks. Where the blood stain speaks. Vengeful ghosts, descend near me.

CURTAIN

ACT IV

Scene 1

A public square. On one side the palace of Imperia all lit up.

VOICE: (outside) Make room for Signor Azzoli, make room.

AZZOLI: (entering) What a success, what a triumph! I've dazzled Venice already with my luxury, and that was at night; what will it be in broad daylight? Everybody rushed to their windows to see me pass, and no one understands that this might be the same Azzoli who was strolling as recently as yesterday with a single lackey! The scrawniest and most shabby of lackeys! Keep these importunates away! Yes, my dear Leone, here's how the miracle works. Two of my uncles who were living in Florence died of the plague in less than an hour and left me a very suitable inheritance that I am just beginning to nibble at. Decidedly, Florence is a charming town, for its palaces and all the uncles who don't need to have another country!

LEONE: So you are rich.

AZZOLI: Enough to wait—

LEONE: Ninetta must be enchanted.

AZZOLI: Not very! I booted her out the door.

LEONE: Bah!

AZZOLI: Now, I must have a mistress with a greater bearing, and Ninetta's turned back nose is an impossible thing.

LEONE: Who are you going to take?

AZZOLI: Fine question! The only woman who might be worthy of me: Imperia!

LEONE: Imperia!

AZZOLI: You find the pretension presumptuous?

LEONE: On the contrary; I'm even sure you will please her a lot. You aren't big, you don't have much beard, but there's a certain charm in your demeanor which seduces women. Even your cough strikes sympathetic notes, and you have an irresistible wink. In a word, you will pass with justice for a very accomplished cavalier.

AZZOLI: (aside) Flatterer! If you are dreaming that I will loan you money for your efforts—

(aloud) So, you approve of me?

LEONE: Sure!

AZZOLI: I intend to emerge from these vulgar intrigues and to give myself immediately the most distinguished relief. Ninetta was only an Italian soubrette, Imperia is a courtesan from Babylon! For example, I must have this cursed Honorius who bothers me a lot drowned or stabbed.

LEONE: You won't have need to rid yourself of him, because Imperia is seeking only a pretext to leave him.

AZZOLI: Right. Women who seek always find.

LEONE: He's refusing her a necklace she wants with all her might.

AZZOLI: Why's he refusing her?

LEONE: In his embarrassment he alleges a thousand motives that are most unlikely to be true, but the true, one-and- only reason is that he lacks the money to pay for the diamonds.

AZOLI: She will have the necklace this very evening. Let's go to her place.

(to his followers) And you, scamps, make the uproar that's suitable to announce me.

ALL: Make way for Signor Azzoli, make way!

(He goes into Imperia's palace. Andronicus enters with Jeppo)

ANDRONICUS: So, Jeppo, you've understood me?

JEPPOA: Perfectly, Milord. And I am ready to execute your orders.

ANDRONICUS: You are certain of being able to get into the Doge's palace unnoticed?

JEPPO: I am sure of it.

ANDRONICUS: This necklace will be placed in her jewel box within an hour?

JEPPO: Yes.

ANDRONICUS: And no one will be able to suspect the hand that put it there?

JEPPO: No one.

ANDRONICUS: So you actually had a fairy for your God-mother?

JEPPO: Not precisely.

ANDRONICUS: Then there has been love under the table.

JEPPO: Milord has guessed it.

ANDRONICUS: The Devil! A woman in a secret is worrisome.

JEPPO: I'll answer for her.

ANDRONICUS: Be careful.

JEPPO: Our accomplice is an honest girl in the service of the Signora, you can count on her discretion as on mine.

ANDRONICUS: I know you, my faithful Jeppo, and I truly believe that you must have chosen well. So, you are sincerely in love?

JEPPO: With all my soul though I am only a poor servant.

ANDRONICUS: When will you marry?

JEPPO: Later, after we've made some savings.

ANDRONICUS: Marry her, I'll dower you.

JEPPO: My dear Lord! Ah, may God make you happy.

ANDRONICUS: (aside) Alas!

(aloud) Go and be prudent; you will find me at home.

(Jeppo leaves)

No question, Honorius is here and I must make a final effort to tear him away from this infinite passion. There's nothing changed in my plans, and the best thing for both of us to do is to leave Venice; I shan't even wait for the arrival of my ships; I'll sell the cargoes in advance; I'll sell all that remains to me, and as soon as I have paid the Jew I will depart for Smyrna. Will I be able to see Ginerva again? What's the use? Tomorrow, as today, I will only be a foreigner for her. Still, what wouldn't I give to witness her joy when she finds the necklace? How was it she knew my name? What difference! I have the strength to leave without seeing her. Once in Smyrna I will try to forget my mad chimera and to cure my dear Honorius. Provided he comes! I feel uneasy, as at the approach of a misfortune!

(explosion of noisy voices at Imperia's)

What's going on in this house? A quarrel? I hear Honorius' voice. He's coming. I will keep myself in readiness to help him if some danger threatens him.

(Andronicus places himself to the side. Imperia and her guests emerge from her palace.)

AZZOLI: (to Honorius) I will go, I tell you, and with this step—

HONORIUS: No, by all the devils!

AZZOLI: And why, if you please?

HONORIUS: Because I forbid you to do it.

AZZOLI: Wow!

IMPERIA: You are unfair, Honorius, to refuse me a gift—failing in your word, so be it! But to prevent another man being more generous, that's a right you haven't got.

HONORIUS: I'm taking that right.

ANDRONICUS: (aside) He must have wine in his head, and his sword won't stay in its scabbard.

HONORIUS: What do you find bad in it?

AZZOLI: To talk like this to the divine Imperia!

HONORIUS: Another word and I'll shorten your ears!

AZZOLI: You are drunk, my dear, learn to drink.

(Honorius half pulls his sword; Ubaldo and Leone stop him)

HONORIUS: Leave me alone.

AZZOLI: Advice from a friend. Orsolo one night threatened me almost the same way. Two hours later he was found in the street struck through the heart.

HONORIUS: You had fought with him?

AZZOLI: I never fight. I have bravos to do that work, just as I have sommeliers to pull my wine. So believe it, I fear no one, not you, not this Andronicus.

ANDRONICUS: (aside) Ah!

AZZOLI: I'm bringing my lackeys and if he won't listen to reason, I'll throw him out the window.

ANDRONICUS: (aside) Truly!

LEONE: Praise God! For the love of Imperia we are all going with you. We ill bring her back the necklace.

ANDRONICUS: (aside) What necklace?

AZZOLI: Let's go.

HONORIUS: Stay. I will go alone.

IMPERIA: (low) Honorius!

(to Honorius) Honorius, this determination proves to me that you still have a little affection for me. Don't get irritated by my demand. Rather, understand my whim. It's not a vile interest that urges me on, and I don't really want more diamonds. I am giving way to an instinct of jealousy. I'm weary of your friendship with Andronicus. I don't intend to share your heart with anyone else. You must be all mine. The mistress must triumph over the friend.

HONORIUS: My head is spinning.

IMPERIA: Go! Go!

HONORIUS: I am running to Andronicus.

ANDRONICUS: (revealing himself) What do you want with me?

HONORIUS: Him!

IMPERIA: (aside) Ah, the struggle will be even more terrible. I am here.

(aloud, to Honorius) Well, it seems the sight of Signor Andronicus intimidates you. What have you done with your impetuous enthusiasm?

HONORIUS: (to Andronicus) Friend, I have a service to ask of you.

ANDRONICUS: If I cam do it for you, count on me.

HONORIUS: Last night you went to Shylock?

ANDRONICUS: Yes.

HONORIUS: You purchased a necklace from him?

ANDRONICUS: Yes.

HONORIUS: Give it to me!

ANDRONICUS: Impossible!

HONORIUS: Because I swore I would have that necklace.

ANDRONICUS: You were wrong.

HONORIUS: I cannot explain your refusal; after all, it's not a question of merchandise. I already owe you a lot; I will owe you a little more. Sell it to me at whatever price you want.

ANDRONICUS: (reproachfully) Oh!

(simply) You couldn't pay as much as it cost me.

HONORIUS: Meaning I am ruined!

ANDRONICUS: No, no. You don't understand correctly.

HONORIUS: Still.

ANDRONICUS: I repeat to you that what you are asking of me is an impossibility.

HONORIUS: I repeat to you that I've sworn to have that necklace.

ANDRONICUS: You weren't in your right mind when you took that oath.

HONORIUS: Heavens, Andronicus, you are the wiser and the more virtuous, I agree; but you are wrong to take on the airs of a tutor, and are forgetting that I am no longer of the age when one receives lessons.

IMPERIA: (to Honorius in a whisper) Very fine!

ANDRONICUS: Your words are hurtful, and it's the first time there's been resentment towards me in your eyes. For certain, I don't wish you ill; you've dined a bit too much, I can indeed say that to you, I'm saying it with a smile. Beware of this fever and wait until your heart calms your head. An hour of rest and the cloud will evaporate. Now you are giving in to a malign influence. We must leave, and as soon as we are alone our hands will rejoin.

IMPERIA: (low to Honorius) If you go away, everything is broken between us.

HONORIUS: I'm staying!

ANDRONICUS: And as for me, I'm withdrawing. Don't you see that we are in a public square and that such a conversation should be isolated and secret?

LEONE: (to Andronicus) A public square? Is that what's bothering you? Hold on. In some places where a joyful group is found, it assumes the good custom of putting itself at its ease as behind four walls. The streets, the squares, the canals, all Venice belongs to us, and I am going to prove to you we are quite at home.

(to lackey) Hola, the rest of you, guard all the exits and drive away with sticks the first wise guy who intends to force his passage. You, Ubaldo, make the proclamation legal at the top of your voice.

UBALDO: My dear fellow citizens, if a lamp remains lit, if a window remains open, the Chevaliers of Imperia will set fire within the hour to your rat holes.

(Lights are extinguished; windows close)

LEONE: (to Andronicus) You see, these simple words have a magic effect. Now let's form a circle, a true closed field.

ANDRONICUS: Is this over? I will tell you that your joke is little to my taste and that I intend to retire.

HONORIUS: You will listen to me.

ANDRONICUS: I pity your weakness.

HONORIUS: For God's sake let's finish this!

ANDRONICUS: Honorius, patience has an end.

HONORIUS: Indeed!

ANDRONICUS: Is that a threat?

HONORIUS: Why are you torturing yourself like this?

ANDRONICUS: He's the one complaining!

HONORIUS: Well, my friend, I still have the right to give you this title. Prove to me that you have serious reasons to keep this necklace, tell me the reason that compels you to refuse me. Confide the secret to me.

ANDRONICUS: No.

HONORIUS: I beg you.

ANDRONICUS: No.

HONORIUS: Why?

ANDRONICUS: Because you are not worthy of it!

HONORIUS: Oh, indeed I recognize that. One is not the friend of a man when one closes his heart to him. Never have I possessed your confidence.

ANDRONICUS: Deserve it today. Take the hand I am offering you; renounce your debauchery and I swear to you I will have nothing hidden from you.

HONORIUS: These conditions offend me. Why are you keeping this necklace?

ANDRONICUS: Follow me if you want to know.

HONORIUS: You will tell me here.

ANDRONICUS: I would sooner die!

HONORIUS: Honor, did you say? Each understands it in his own way. Yet once more; I've sworn to have those diamonds and I will keep my word. You shall not leave.

ANDRONICUS: You want me to blow up in the end. Shylock is a usurer, a miscreant, a Jew. He dishonors the commerce of Venice; he sews ruin on this path, he's unaware of pity, he insults to tears and laughs at despair, Shylock is a monstrous combination of hate and cupidity; Shylock is the image of the Demon! Well his accursed hand has less soiled that necklace than would than hand of this ruined woman!

HONORIUS: By heaven!

IMPERIA: You are a gentleman, Honorius, and I've been insulted in front of you! And you do not feel that it's your face that has been slapped!

(Honorius puts his sword in his hand)

HONORIUS: On guard!

ANDRONICUS: Wretch!

HONORIUS: On guard!

ANDRONICUS: Twenty years of friendship!

HONORIUS: Chimera!

ANDRONICUS: Honorius, this is caused by delirium.

HONORIUS: I know that well.

ANDRONICUS: Come to yourself.

HONORIUS: You don't argue with madmen, you fight them.

ANDRONICUS: Never!

HONORIUS: Defend yourself, or—

ANDRONICUS: The sword that saved your life will never be used except to defend mine.

HONORIUS: Let's go!

(They fight)

AZZOLI: (aside) If only they'd skewer each other.

(Honorius is disarmed.)

HONORIUS: What's happened? A cloud's evaporated. A light has crossed through my skull. Andronicus, this sword—

IMPERIA: Take it up, Honorius, or I will find other arms

to avenge me. Help me!

LEONE: We are here.

ANDRONICUS: Come on, then! I defy you all by myself!

HONORIUS: Ah!

(leaping for his sword, he grasps it and places himself beside Andronicus) Now there will be two of us!

ANDRONICUS: Get back, knights of debauchery and orgy!

(A confused battle, some patricians resist weakly, others try to flee)

Honorius, use the flat of the sword.

(the two friends end by sweeping them out. Honorius kneels to Andronicus who raises him up)

Friend, you can hear me now! I refused you the necklace because I love the Doge's daughter.

HONORIUS: Andronicus, I don't yet deserve your pardon, but I intend to regain it. I'm leaving Venice, I'm going to fight the pirates of the Adriatic, and you won't see me again until the day I become worthy of you.

ANDRONICUS: My friend, my brother!

HONORIUS: Goodbye!

(he throws himself into the arms of Andronicus)

CURTAIN

ACT IV

Scene 2

Ginerva's room in the Palace of the Doge.

GINERVA: So, Fabia, you want to get married?

FABIA: Yes, Madame.

GINERVA: I consent to it gladly, my dear Fabia. Who are you going to marry?

FABIA: Jeppo.

GINERVA: Who is this Jeppo?

FABER: A good and faithful servant of Signor Andronicus.

GINERVA: The merchant of Smyrna?

FABIA: Yes, Madame.

GINERVA: I needn't ask if you love your fiancé?

FABIA: To complete my joy his master is dowering him.

GINERVA: Ah, that's fine! As for the rest, nothing surprises me about him; no one possesses a more just title to the general esteem, and in doing good deeds he hardly leaves anything to glean after him. This young man is very rich is he not?

FABIA: Immensely.

GINERVA: As for me, Fabia, I am poor, although I dwell in a magnificent palace and my father is Doge of Venice.

FABIA: Madame.

GINERVA: Your husband must make you happy. You deserve it.— Is my father in?

FABIA: Shut in with that villainous Jew who's going to give him money.

GINERVA: Shylock kept his word.

FABIA: Your toilette is finished, Madame.

GINERVA: Fine. Go find your Jeppo.

FABIA: Ah, I was forgetting.

GINERVA: What?

FABIA: Your necklace.

GINERVA: Alas.

FABIA: Where is your jewel box?

GINERVA: On the table, Fabia, but it's empty.

FABIA: It's not empty.

GINERVA: What are you saying?

FABIA: Here's the necklace.

GINERVA: My necklace! My dear necklace. Yes, this is it, it's really it. How did it get back in my hands? Fabia, Fabia, speak will you! You know nothing? What's it matter, here it is, I am pressing it to my lips. Oh, I laugh, I weep, I am mad with joy. It's a dream, a fairy tale. My childhood has returned. I'm ten years old. I'm running on the lawn, my mother is still alive, everything is full of flowers and rays of light. With this talisman, I defy misfortune. My father often told me: "You are courageous and strong." No, no, I am only a weak girl and my heart overflows! But I am thinking: there's only one father who can cause such surprises. No doubt about it, the Doge was touched by my sorrow, he repurchased the necklace, he replaced it in this jewel box during my sleep. Oh, I am in a hurry to see him, to embrace him.

(calling) Father, father!

FABIA: (aside) Let's avoid questions.

(she leaves)

DOGE: (entering) You called me?

GINERVA: Oh, thanks, thanks.

DOGE: What do I see?

GINERVA: Yes. You are pretending astonishment but it's useless. I know everything.

DOGE: Who returned it to you?

GINERVA: You.

DOGE: You are mistaken.

GINERVA: Why this mystery?

DOGE: On my honor, I am unaware how this necklace got here.

GINERVA: It was in the jewel box.

DOGE: That's strange.

GINERVA: Indeed.

DOGE: Ah, the Jew may be able to tell us.

(raising his voice) Come in, Shylock, come in.

SHYLOCK: (entering) Well, Signora, you must be happy.

GINERVA: You know then?

SHYLOCK: No question.

GINERVA: Shylock, we were wrong to think you evil. You had pity on my tears, and it was you who returned it to me.

SHYLOCK: These young girls have such romantic heads.

GINERVA: Oh, if you did this.

SHYLOCK: I am incapable of such a beautiful deed.

DOGE: Why, then—.

SHYLOCK: Why, what astonishes you, Milord? I am not a business man for nothing. I bought these diamonds and I resold them, that's all.

DOGE: You resold them?

SHYLOCK: Yesterday evening.

GINERVA: To whom?

SHYLOCK: To a handsome, cavalier, signora. I will confess he paid dearly for them.

DOGE: His name?

SHYLOCK: Pardon me, I hesitate to tell you. I'm afraid of being indiscreet.

DOGE: Reply!

SHYLOCK: All the same, it was not agreed, I'd keep quiet about it; still to name a purchaser, it's praising him.

DOGE: In the end.

SHYLOCK: The handsome cavalier, the generous cavalier is called Andronicus.

GINERVA: (aside) Him.

(she replaces the necklace in the jewel box)

DOGE: Andronicus! What motive?

SHYLOCK: Ah, I'm unaware.

DOGE: Is it true you are unaware of it?

SHYLOCK: Oh, I can guess it. Milord, allows me to speak frankly?

DOGE: Speak.

SHYLOCK: I don't like Andronicus, but I will do him justice. He's a virtuous young man, solely concerned with commerce and philanthropy, who would give a soul of character and idealism the same attention as business affairs; madness, surely, but respectable madness. He flees the pleasures of his youth, scorns ephemeral bonds and seeks solitude with pride. To a choice heart like his, a vulgar love could not suffice. Thus, Andronicus chose unhesitatingly the purest, most noble, the living image of his dreams. He adores the mysterious idol in silence and God alone has seen him burn incense in the shadow of the night. When I say God alone, I am mistaken, the Demon, that's what he called me, has also glimpsed the sacrosanct flame. Yesterday was the day the veil fell at the moment when the Signora agreed with me about her necklace, with such touching sorrow.

DOGE: Enough!

GINERVA: (aside) He loves me!

SHYLOCK: All the same, I affirm nothing. I am only making a supposition. But, if the Doge wants to be completely enlightened nothing is easier. I've noticed our guilty man on the Rialto often casting glances this way, If your Lordship consents to receive him, I'll go down as quickly as my old legs will permit.

DOGE: Go!

GINERVA: Father!

SHYLOCK: (aside) This affair is in a good way. The father indulgent, the daughter upset, the lover passionate. Now there's a perfect trio! Let's marry these children, let's marry them.

(he leaves)

DOGE: How pale you are.

GINERVA: That Jew scares me.

DOGE: You have nothing to fear from him. I am still master and I will render his hate impotent. But Andronicus is going to come. Do you want to withdraw?

GINERVA: Why? That would be bad! Don't I owe him thanks? I would be wrong to flee a man who never offended me as if he were an enemy.

DOGE: And if what Shylock says is true?

GINERVA: That affection honors me.

(Andronicus appears) Why, here he is.

ANDRONICUS: (aside) Ah. That infamous Shylock!

DOGE: Come closer, Andronicus!

ANDRONICUS: Pardon me, Milord. I snatched this precious necklace from the hands of the Jew, but you ought to be unaware of it still.

DOGE: Better that we know it so as not to be ingrates.

ANDRONICUS: Why did that cursed monster speak?

DOGE: You have no need to blush for a good deed.

ANDRONICUS: A good deed!

GINERVA: Yes, that's the word. You wouldn't doubt it if you had been witness to my joy when I rediscovered my treasure. Now it's to you that I ask, can I keep this necklace?

ANDRONICUS: Madame.

GINERVA: Speak frankly. Whatever your reply may be, it will be that of a man of honor, and I submit to it in advance.

ANDRONICUS: You can, because it is a dying man that offers it to you.

DOGE: Andronicus.

GINERVA: What are you saying?

ANDRONICUS: To depart is to die, and I am going to

leave Venice forever. Keep this supreme gift as a feeble thanks of the protection and esteem with which your noble father has always honored me.

GINERVA: (taking the necklace) You see, I obey.

DOGE: You are leaving?

ANDRONICUS: I am returning to Smyrna this very day, Milord, momentarily. There are business affairs which re-call me there. I was awaiting two ships from the Indies on which are found the better part of my fortune. And that is what has prevented me from leaving sooner. But, at the moment in which Your Lordship called me, they signaled entry into the port. The values they bring me are consider-able, and I bitterly regret they didn't arrive yesterday for you would not have had need of Shylock. In the end there are men whose star is bad and I am of their number. What can be done about it? Be resigned.

DOGE: You never mentioned this departure to me.

ANDRONICUS: What was the use? Receive my good-byes.

GINERVA: All my gratitude to you.

ANDRONICUS: (aside) All my soul to you!

DOGE: Is it true you will never come back?

ANDRONICUS: Never.

(the Doge offers him his hand)

Ah, I thought to be a man, and I am only a child. Thanks, Milord, thanks.

DOGE: My friend, my son!

ANDRONICUS: Your son, me!

(looking at Ginerva) What did I see? No, I'm not mistaken, it's not a diamond fallen from her necklace, it's a tear fallen from her eye. Oh, a tear of hers. Oh, reply, reply. Even if you must drive me away now Is it for the one who's leaving that you shed it?

GINERVA: Yes, I regret you like a brother.

ANDRONICUS: Don't weep any more then, for you are breaking my heart. Like a brother! Oh, that affection does not suffice me. I've dared to love you, I dare to say it. My audacity is complete now. I admit my love before you, before your father; I would confess it before God himself., if he threatened me with his thunder. I've loved you honestly, clearly, but without hope. For I must leave, and I was imposing an eternal absence on myself. Chance alone has joined us and I didn't seek this interview. Whatever it may be, my life is in your hands, a word, a gesture, a look of yours could change my destiny; I await it, I implore it.— Nothing! Nothing!

DOGE: (low to Ginerva) My child, why are you turning your head away, why are you keeping silent? I've read your heart and I am happy to know that Andronicus is worthy of you. His birth is equal to ours, and it's to work, to probity that he owes his riches.

GINERVA: His riches! Yes, Lord Andronicus is generous.

ANDRONICUS: (to Ginerva) Must I still leave?

GINERVA: Yes.

ANDRONICUS: Goodbye, Madame!

SHYLOCK: (off) Don't they understand each other here?

DOGE: What have you done?

GINERVA: My duty.

ANDRONICUS: Goodbye.

DOGE: (to Shylock) Who sent for you?

SHYLOCK: No one, Milord, no one. It's because I have such important news for my colleague Andronicus.

ANDRONICUS: For me?

SHYLOCK: Two ships just entered the port. Two superb ships recently bedecked, refitted to the nines which in this fine weather majestically cleave the blue waves of the Adriatic. There's a crowd there to admire them like on days of grand feasts.

ANDRONICUS: I know that.

SHYLOCK: Magnificent vessels.

ANDRONICUS: They are mine.

SHYLOCK: Oh, yours? Not completely. That is to say they belong to Genoese Captains and you only charted them for the voyage to the Indies.

ANDRONICUS: What's that matter? The cargo—

SHYLOCK: Here's where I'm ahead of you. All that shines is not gold and nothing is so proud as appearances.

ANDRONICUS: What's that mean?

SHYLOCK: It means that these admirable ships are empty.

ADRONICUS: What do you mean?

SHYLOCK: Like the hollow of my hand. They were pillaged by Pirates on the coasts of Africa.

ANDRONICUS: You lie!

SHYLOCK: It's ruin for you.

DOGE: Ruin?

SHYLOCK: I think so.

GINERVA: Ruin, you said! (to Andronicus) Poverty renders us equal; here's my hand.

ANDRONICUS: Is this possible?

GINERVA: I will console you, I will love you! I do love you.

ANDRONICUS: Ginerva!

GINERVA: Are you pleased with me, Papa?

DOGE: (opening his arms to her) Yes, and I thank God again, who mixes a smile with our tears.

SHYLOCK: (aside) Fine!

ANDRONICUS: Ah! Blessed be this disaster!

SHYLOCK: (low to Andronicus) Still, don't forget those sixty-thousand sequins.

ANDRONICUS: (low to Shylock) You will be paid.

SHYLOCK: I'm counting on it.

ANDRONICUS: I have a month!

SHYLOCK: Pardon, my young master. You have only twenty-nine days.

CURTAIN

ACT V

The Scene is the same as the third act.

AT RISE, Shylock is seated at a table staring at a sandglass. Jacob is standing near a door and seems to listen worriedly to noises outside.

SHYLOCK: Flow, then cursed sand, flow, will you! More quickly! More quickly! O inflexible slowness of time!

JACOB: I am not deceived. The crowd is massing on the Jewish quarter.

SHYLOCK: The time allowed has not expired. But Andronicus cannot escape me again. If he had found the sum he owes me he would have already come to cover this table with sequins, and say to me "Shylock return my note to me!" Barely a few moments. Yes, this is a century of torture. Oh, how I would give all my treasure to accelerate the movement of this sand!

JACOB: Those noises are beginning to worry me.

SHYLOCK: And if I were going to die, suddenly, thunderstruck! Look, look, calm down! What to do to deceive this horrible hope? What to do? Sharpen my knife? No, I am not obliged there; it's not specified in the note.

JACOB: The Christians have no doubt learned that Shylock wants to kill Andronicus. Decidedly, I have to warn him.

(approaching Shylock) Master!

SHYLOCK: (violently) What do you want?

JACOB: Master!

SHYLOCK: Has someone knocked on the door?

JACOB: No, but—

SHYLOCK: You are sure of it?

JACOB: I beg you to listen to me.

SHYLOCK: (eye on the sand glass) Wait, wait. Ah, the hour is past, the credit is exactable, and it's no longer in gold that Andronicus will pay me.

JACOB: You still want to kill him?

SHYLOCK: Kill him? It's only a question of my having a right to a pound of flesh, that's all! I will cut it from his breast and if he doesn't die of it, so much the worse for him! Oh, I will do it with the best faith possible; my hand is firm, my glance is exact, and I won't take an ounce more or an ounce less. We could take a scales.

JACOB: But the Christian's note is null!

SHYLOCK: Come on! The note is bizarre, extravagant, unheard of, so be it! It's the result of a ferocious vengeance. Indeed, I want it; but it was written honestly, and signed freely, that is all that is important; the rest concerns no one. I have my own way of understanding business, if others do not approve of it, don't buy from me, if you buy from me, pay me. Thus, Andronicus will pay. I didn't have the power to impose this bargain, but he did. So much the worse for him.

JACOB: The law of Venice condemns to a terrible death the Jew who sheds the blood of a Christian, so by striking that man, you will deliver yourself to the executioner.

SHYLOCK: That's my affair, Jacob. Let's not discuss it any further. I have the right to a pound of flesh, it belongs to me, I want it, I shall have it. I swore it to myself, I swore it in the face of heaven, on the Holy Sabbath day, and you actually think that I will perjure myself, in conscience!

JACOB: Listen. Reprisals have begun already. You don't even have time for vengeance.

SHYLOCK: Let the dogs howl. My walls are thick, my doors solid!

JACOB: They are trying to set fire.

SHYLOCK: Iron and steel don't burn. Don't tremble like that. Our excellent Doge who protects foreigners doing business in Venice is going to send police to sweep away the populace.

JACOB: Ah, here they are.

SHYLOCK: Yes, I hear the clash of arms.

JACOB: The shouting is diminishing, the populace is fleeing.

SHYLOCK: Go see, go see!

(Jacob leaves)

If he doesn't come now, if his integrity weakens, if love has rendered him cowardly! To sacrifice everything for such a vengeance and not to get it! O what fever! What fever! My head is exploding and I see red waves rolling before my eyes. I'm thirsty, passionately thirsty. Help, me Jacob, help me. I need to drink, my throat's on fire. Water! No, no, not water. Blood!

JACOB: He's here.

SHYLOCK: Who? Who? Who?

JACOB: Andronicus.

SHYLOCK: O honest young man! Leave us, Jacob. Go fill your pockets and flee with the others.

(Jacob gestures in protest) Go, will you, sensitive heart.

(Jacob leaves by one door, Andronicus enters by another.)

SHYLOCK: I am alone at last, alone with my victim, and every drop of his blood belongs to me! Let's resume the calm of a creditor, and let's be no more than a calm merchant in his counting house.

ANDRONICUS: (approaching) Shylock.

SHYLOCK: Ah, it's you, my young master. You've come for a certain note that you subscribed to a month ago.

ANDRONICUS: The street is cleared; the police that I brought with me are surrounding your house; you are safe and we can speak without fear of being interrupted.

SHYLOCK: I think that we don't have much to say to each other.

ANDRONICUS: I owe you sixty thousand sequins.

SHYLOCK: Meaning you did owe me them. The hour for

payment has passed.

ANDRONICUS: In the end, I've been able to gather only half that sum.

SHYLOCK: Thirty thousand sequins?

ANDRONICUS: They are at your disposition.

SHYLOCK: You were obliged to pay me sixty. Sixty is what I need.

ANDRONICUS: But I don't have them.

SHYLOCK: Luckily for me, I foresaw what would happen and I still find myself sufficiently protected. You will be quits for paying me in the other manner.

ANDRONICUS: You won't exact that horrible debt.

SHYLOCK: Would you like me to read the note to you?

ANDRONICUS: Listen, Shylock. I cannot purchase more dearly this necklace, and I do not repent of what I've done. I won't argue the engagement I made towards you, and nothing in the world would push me into denying it, because it's not only with my hand that I signed it, it is with my honor! Thus, I am prepared for everything. My heart is not accessible to fear, and, you see, I came without arms.

SHYLOCK: You will carry away the esteem of Shylock.

ANDRONICUS: Think that you are nearing the tomb and that you will soon appear before the Supreme Judge.

SHYLOCK: The note bears—

ANDRONICUS: Up to now, happiness has never smiled on me, but today, the Sun shone. Love came and I cling to life!

SHYLOCK: I know that perfectly well. That entered my calculations.

ANDRONICUS: Ginerva! Ginerva!

SHYLOCK: Hold on, young man. Let's get this over with. We are wasting precious time.

ANDRONICUS: Trying to move Shylock, it's like trying to ask the Ocean not to roar during a storm.

SHYLOCK: Now you are right about that.

ANDRONICUS: So you intend to kill me.

SHYLOCK: I intend to be paid with my own hands.

ANDRONICUS: (aside) Ginerva! Forgive the one who's going to die worthy of your love, and faithful to his honor! To you also, a last thought, dear Honorius. Battle valiantly for Venice and triumph over its enemies!

SHYLOCK: Well?

ANDRONICUS: I am ready.

SHYLOCK: (aside) Strength of my old body, concentrate yourself entirely in this eye and hand! You, my son, receive this sacrifice, and shiver with joy in your unknown tomb.

ANDRONICUS: Strike, will you.

SHYLOCK: (raising the knife)

HONORIUS: (outside) Shylock, Andronicus!

(entering) Stop, Shylock, stop! God be praised I've arrived in time.

ANDRONICUS: Honorius! Then I can shake your hand before dying!

HONORIUS: You shall not die!

SHYLOCK: Begone, cursed, begone!

HONORIUS: Cast away that knife.

SHYLOCK: No!

HONORIUS: Cast away that knife with horror!

SHYLOCK: Stop, young fool!

HONORIUS: Because—

SHYLOCK: I intend to strike!

HONORIUS: (dragging him aside) He's your son!

(Shylock lets his knife fall and recoils, shocked. Honorius stops Andronicus with a gesture.)

SHYLOCK: My son, my son—

HONORIUS: Here's the proof.

(he gives him a parchment that Shylock reads avidly)

The leader of the pirates that I defeated was this Arnheim who carried off your son twenty years ago. Arnheim, as he was dying, signed this confession to his crime.

SHYLOCK: (with joy) Yes, it's him.

(he rushes towards Andronicus; Honorius holds him back)

HONORIUS: To recognize him is to ruin him.

(uproar outside)

ANDRONICUS: The Doge, Ginerva.

HONORIUS: The son of the Jew, Shylock will never become the spouse of Ginerva, the Christian.

SHYLOCK: Yes, that's true. Never!

GINERVA: (outside) Andronicus! Where is he?

(she enters with the Doge and throws herself into the arms of Andronicus)

Living! Saved!

DOGE: Shylock spared him.

SHYLOCK: Yes, Milord. Hate is impious and the plans of God are terrible.

GINERVA: What is it then that changed your heart?

SHYLOCK: Heaven made a miracle, Signora.

DOGE: A miracle.

SHYLOCK: Yes.

DOGE: What is this document on which your eyes are fixed with tenderness?

SHYLOCK: It's proof that my son exists.

GINERVA: Your son?

SHYLOCK: And I—

HONORIUS: (to Shylock) Be careful.

SHYLOCK: And I'm going to find him again.

DOGE: Where is he?

SHYLOCK: Oh, far, quite far from Venice. It's my secret.

(aside) Yes, I'll have to leave because my soul would betray itself. Leave, leave, when he is there, near me, when I would only have to stretch my arms out to him, to scream to him "I love you." Yes, I will have the courage, I will accomplish the duty, that's my punishment! And yet, I won't have long to suffer!

(aloud) Goodbye, Milord, goodbye all. I am leaving Venice, never to return.

(looking at Honorius) Never!

(to Andronicus) Grant me a grace. Allow me to touch your hand. Oh, hold on. I demand this grace on my knees.

GINERVA: (terrified) Andronicus!

(she places herself between Shylock and Andronicus)

SHYLOCK: Don't be alarmed, Signora. I am no longer to be feared.

(to Andronicus) Would you?

ANDRONICUS: (giving him his hand) Here it is!

SHYLOCK: And you forgive me?

ANDRONICUS: Yes.

SHYLOCK: Oh!

(he covers Andronicus's hand with kisses and tears.)

ANDRONICUS: (aside) His sorrow makes me ill.

HONORIUS: (aside) Is he going to weaken?

SHYLOCK: And now, goodbye forever. Of all my treasures amassed by usury I'm taking with me only this traveling stick.

(aside) The flaming sword is driving me from Eden. Unquenched loved, come into exile to devour the heart of old Shylock.

(to Andronicus and Ginerva) Be happy! Be blessed!

CURTAIN